EMPIRE AND REVOLUTION

A socialist history of the First World War

Dave Sherry

About the author

Dave Sherry lives in Glasgow and is a retired public sector housing worker and trade union activist. He is the author of *Occupy! A Short History of Workers' Occupations* (Bookmarks 2010) and *John Maclean: Red Clydesider* (Bookmarks 2014). He is a member of the Socialist Workers Party.

EMPIRE AND REVOLUTION

A socialist history of the First World War

Dave Sherry

Bookmarks *Publications*

Empire and Revolution:
A socialist history of the First World War
Dave Sherry
Published 2014 by Bookmarks Publications
c/o 1 Bloomsbury Street, London WC1B 3QE
© Bookmarks Publications
Designed and typeset by Peter Robinson
Printed by Melita Press
Cover picture: British West Indies
Regiment troops in France, 1916.
© Imperial War Museum.
ISBN print edition: 978 1 909026 629
ISBN kindle: 978 1 909026 636
ISBN e-pub: 978 1 909026 643
ISBN PDF: 978 1 909026 650

Contents

Introduction:
The present is history

In Britain there is an attempt by government ministers, commentators and historians to reinvent the First World War as a time when the whole nation rallied against an external enemy and triumphed; a time when "we were all in it together" fighting for "democracy and freedom". This is a travesty of history.

The First World War was the greatest barbarism the world had ever seen. It was a clash of empires in which each of the rival ruling classes was prepared for any number of dead to advance their imperial interests. It provoked mutinies, mass resistance and a wave of revolutionary struggle, which brought it to an abrupt end in November 1918, toppling monarchies and dissolving empires in the process.

Throughout 1919 Britain came closer to socialist revolution than at any time before or since. Its empire plunged into crisis as British military authority crumbled in the face of rebellion in Ireland, Egypt, Iraq, India, China and the West Indies.

In August 2014 the centenary of the outbreak of the First World War coincides with the hosting of the Commonwealth Games in Glasgow and the final countdown to the Scottish independence referendum in September. Prime Minister David Cameron has made it clear he will use all of these events to promote militarism and a reactionary British nationalism—partly to pander to anti-immigrant sentiment but also to keep Scotland in the union.

Glasgow's merchants—like their counterparts in Britain's other western seaports, Liverpool and Bristol—made vast fortunes from slavery and empire. Their ill-gotten gains laid the basis for Glasgow's emergence as "the Second City of Empire" and a key munitions hub for the British state and its war profiteers; together they bear responsibility for the slaughter that began in 1914.

Against the present attempt to whitewash militarism and empire stands the tradition of working class resistance. The explosion of working class revolt during the First World War brought to prominence Britain's two finest Marxists, James Connolly and John Maclean.

They led the opposition to the war because they understood it was about repartitioning the world between the great powers and that it would lead to further imperialist conflict. Like Lenin in Russia they anticipated the importance of national liberation struggles in the colonies and how they could weaken the British Empire and imperialism in general.

Connolly was executed by a British firing squad for his part in leading the Dublin Easter Rising in 1916. Maclean was imprisoned on five separate occasions by the British state; twice condemned to lengthy terms of penal servitude for sedition, twice he was released through mass protest. Maclean was only 44 when he died in 1923—his death hastened by the hunger strikes, forced feeding and harsh treatment he endured in prison. Ten thousand Glaswegians lined the streets for his funeral.

A warning of what lies ahead

The First World War should be viewed not as a historical curiosity or a matter for academic dispute, but as a powerful reminder of how war and empire are rooted in capitalist competition and a warning of what may lie ahead in the new imperialism of the 21st century.

A BBC TV debate on the "Great War" between two Tory historians, Niall Ferguson and Max Hastings, ignored this. Despite being given a generous primetime TV slot, neither of them connected the First World War with the world of today. Their "was it a necessary or unnecessary war" argument begged the question, necessary for whom? The 20 million human beings it killed and the millions wounded and maimed? That the First World War might have political consequences today seems to have escaped the BBC programme planners. This is astonishing, given that the war decisively shaped the 20th century and weighs heavily on the present. The 21st century began with geopolitical rivalries and tensions between the present-day superpowers, which have set proxy wars in motion reminiscent of those in the build-up to 1914.

The First World War followed a series of regional wars—the Boer War of 1899-1902, the Russo-Japanese War of 1904 and the Balkan Wars of 1912-13. Yet Karl Kautsky, the leading thinker in pre-war European social democracy, had argued that as capitalism developed it would become more benign, reducing the tendency to war.

That myth is still around today, expressed in the claim that globalisation and the end of the Cold War would bring "a peace dividend". Yet we have witnessed the opposite. Every day on the TV news we see war or the threat of war, as the dominant powers jostle with each other for influence by supporting different sides in regional conflicts.

The 20th century ended with a re-run of the Balkan conflict that preceded 1914, with France, Germany and the US backing different sides in the break-up of former Yugoslavia. In 1999 Nato bombers pounded the towns and cities of Serbia, Montenegro and Kosovo, flouting the United Nations and exacerbating tension with China and Russia, who opposed the bombings.

The Project for the New American Century—the invasions

of Afghanistan and Iraq at the start of this century and the threat to attack Iran—was about American capitalism stamping its authority on the world. Despite Bush's "shock and awe", the neo-cons failed in their aims and the US state has been looking for ways to reverse the setbacks it suffered when it occupied those countries and set fire to the Middle East.

That is why the US encouraged Israel to attack Lebanon in 2006, Ethiopia to attack Somalia in 2007 and Georgia to attack Russia's borders in 2008—an act which not only sharpened the tensions between Nato and Russia, but also widened the divisions *among* Nato member states.

Similar predatory manoeuvring has been taking place in Central Africa, where Chinese influence is growing; around the civil war in Syria; and across the wider Middle East. As I write, the same imperialist brinkmanship is being played out in the Ukraine and the Crimean Peninsula.

As with the Balkans, rival imperial powers have fought to control the Ukraine for centuries. Take Lviv, the main city in western Ukraine. In 1914 it was Lemberg, capital of the Austro-Hungarian province of Galicia. Between 1919 and 1939 it was Lwow, second city of Poland. It then became Lvov in the Soviet Republic of the Ukraine after the Second World War.

Since the collapse of the Soviet Union, Ukraine's rulers have been trying to balance between Russia, Europe and the US. What began as a battle between two gangs of corrupt and thuggish oligarchs—one aligned with Putin's Russia, the other with the US and the EU—has now been overtaken by international rivalry with the big imperial powers seeking to extend their spheres of influence.

This is exactly what happened in the build up to 1914. The continuing role of imperialism makes it crucial that we have a clear understanding of the First World War.

I

Why the world went to war

"My father was a soldier in the Great War, fighting in the trenches of France because of a shot fired in a city he'd never heard of called Sarajevo. And when he died at the age of 93, I inherited his campaign medals. One of them depicts a winged Victory and on the obverse side is depicted the words: 'The Great War for Civilisation'.

I used to argue—hopelessly I'm sure—that every reporter should carry a history book in his back pocket. In 1992 I was in Sarajevo and once, as Serbian shells whizzed over my head, I stood upon the very paving stone upon which Gavrilo Princip stood as he fired the fatal shot that sent my father to the trenches in the First World War. And of course the shots were still being fired in Sarajevo in 1992, the year in which my father died. It was as if history was a gigantic echo chamber."

—*Robert Fisk*[1]

August 2014 is the centenary of the outbreak of the First World War—the greatest organised slaughter the world had yet seen. No previous war had been so brutal or so vast in scale. Latest estimates are that 10 million were killed and another 20 million wounded in the fighting, while at least 10 million civilians died as a consequence of the war.[2]

Long before 1914, Europe's ruling classes knew the continent was heading to war—and so did the leaders of the European socialist movement. Yet very few individuals really grasped what it would be like, how long it would last or where it would lead.

One of those who did was Karl Marx's great friend and collaborator, Friedrich Engels. In 1887 he envisaged:

A world war of an extent and violence hitherto undreamt of. Eight to ten million soldiers will slaughter each other and devour the whole of Europe until they have stripped it barer than any swarm of locusts has ever done.

The devastation of the Thirty Years War compressed into three or four years and spread over the whole continent; famine, pestilence, general demoralisation both of armies and of the mass of the people, produced by acute distress; chaos in our trade, industry, commerce and credit, ending in general bankruptcy; collapse of the old states to such an extent that crowns will roll on the pavements and there will be nobody to pick them up; absolute impossibility of foreseeing how this will all end and who will be the victors; only one result absolutely certain; general exhaustion and the creation of the conditions for the final victory of the working class.

This is the prospect when the system of mutual outbidding in armaments, taken to its final extreme, at last bears its inevitable fruits. This my lords, princes and statesmen is where in your wisdom you have brought old Europe.[3]

So much of what Engels wrote came true. The outcome of the war did nothing to solve the crisis that produced it. The European revolution that it provoked brought the slaughter to an end and forced the armistice of 1918, but the workers' movement was contained and eventually defeated.

The Versailles Settlement of 1919—the peace conference that was supposed to set up a new international order—repartitioned the world in such a way that it laid the basis for an even bloodier war 20 years later. The fault lines established then still destabilise the world of today.

"The Great War for Civilisation"—the lie engraved on

Empire and Revolution

the British Victory Medal—has long been condemned as a futile slaughter. In the final paragraph of his book, *The Pity of War*, Tory historian Niall Ferguson concludes: "The First World War was at once piteous, in the poet's sense, and 'a pity'. It was something worse than a tragedy, something we are taught by theatre to regard as unavoidable. It was the greatest *error* of modern history".[4]

One in ten British men under age 45 were killed or badly wounded and the British casualty rate was by no means the worst. The anti-war socialist Rosa Luxemburg, writing in Germany six weeks after the war had begun, counted its mounting cost:

> The cannon fodder that was loaded upon the trains in August and September is rotting on the battlefields of Belgium and the Vosges while profits are sprouting like weeds, from the fields of the dead... Shamed, dishonoured, wading in blood and dripping with filth, thus capitalist society stands...as a roaring beast, as an orgy of anarchy, as a pestilential breath devastating culture and humanity.[5]

After four years of carnage the beast devoured up to 20 million lives. There is near universal agreement that 1914 was "something worse than a tragedy" but it is a different matter when it comes to deciding what caused it. In the run-up to the August centenary it seems as if there have been enough books written on the First World War to fill a library. Along with the accompanying television and radio programmes, the great majority of the literature produced is dominated by two explanations.

Was the carnage an avoidable diplomatic error as many historians, including Niall Ferguson, now claim? Was it instead "a necessary war", caused by an aggressive German militarism that could not be appeased, as a host of military historians such as Max Hastings continue to argue? Or is there another explanation?

A necessary war?

One of the two dominant explanations for the First World War, that responsibility lies with Germany and its allies, is as old and tired as the war itself. It is the explanation that shaped the Versailles Settlement of 1919, when history was written by the victors. As part of BBC TV's predictable build up to the August centenary, war historian Max Hastings was given an hour-long programme to argue that the First World War was neither futile nor avoidable but a "necessary war". Here is the argument from another military historian in the same camp, Gary Sheffield:

> Britain went to war with Germany in August 1914 for similar reasons to those for which the country fought Hitler's Germany in the Second World War; to prevent an authoritarian, militarist, expansionist enemy achieving hegemony in Europe and imperilling British security... Whoever started it, the fact was that in 1914 Germany waged a war of aggression that conquered large tracts of its neighbours' territory. As has often been pointed out, there were distinct continuities between the policy of Imperial Germany and its Nazi successor.[6]

Sheffield's attempt to equate the First and Second World Wars does not stand up to scrutiny. Whatever the truth of it, the Second World War is still seen as a war to defeat fascism. The First World War had no such merit. The depiction of pre-war Germany as militarist, expansionist and imperialist is of course true, but what about British imperialism? There are good reasons why the Union Jack came to be known as the butcher's apron. By 1914, Britain had spent 200 years grabbing an empire the German ruling class could only dream of.

The exploitation of India began with the British East India Company in the 1750s and all subsequent attempts at resistance were put down by military force. British ministers of the day boasted that their approach was based on the key principle of the Roman Empire, "divide et impera"—divide and rule. By 1850 British domination extended throughout the whole sub-continent. In 1857 the first Indian War of Independence—"the Indian Mutiny" as the British ruling class prefer to call it—was crushed with ruthless barbarity. In 1919 at Amritsar British troops opened fire on a peaceful crowd, killing 500 and wounding 2,000.

Across the globe Britannia waived the rules. When Kitchener's army conquered Sudan at the battle of Omdurman in 1898, his machine-gunners killed 10,000 Sudanese with the loss of only 48 men. In the aftermath of the battle prisoners and the wounded were shot and bayoneted. Kitchener had the skull of the Sudanese leader turned into an inkstand.

In South Africa Britain pioneered concentration camps during the Boer War. In Ireland, Britain's oldest colony, the British war cabinet ordered the violent suppression of the 1916 Easter Rising and the summary execution of its leadership by firing squad, including the anti-war socialist James Connolly. The Commander of the British Forces at the time, General Sir John Maxwell, had supervised the slaughter of the Sudanese at Omdurman 18 years earlier.

Compared to Britain, the Kaiser's Germany was a mere novice at imperialism.

The second of the dominant explanations for 1914 is presented in Christopher Clark's *The Sleepwalkers: How Europe Went to War in 1914*. Well researched, his book successfully demolishes the claim that Germany and its allies were mainly responsible: "this does not mean that we should minimise the belligerence and imperialist paranoia of the Austrian and German policy makers... But the Germans were not the only imperialists and not the only ones to succumb to paranoia".[7]

This is far preferable to the lazy, anti-German narrative,

but Christopher Clark's conclusion sidesteps the question of cause and responsibility altogether. There are "too many complexities, too many agencies" for a single root cause or culprit to be fingered:

> The outbreak of war in 1914 is not an Agatha Christie drama at the end of which we will discover the culprit, standing over the corpse, in the conservatory with a smoking pistol... Viewed in this light the outbreak of war was a tragedy, not a crime... The protagonists were sleepwalkers, watchful but unseeing, haunted by dreams, yet blind to the reality of the horror they were about to bring into the world.[8]

The critics all praise the supposed balance and subtlety of Christopher Clark's conclusion, yet he absolves the economic system which drove Europe into catastrophe. To explain away 1914 as a one-off accident, an unintended disaster, is to whitewash or ignore the bellicose nature of capitalism.

The war was a tragedy *and* a crime. What Clark describes as a series of blind, irrational, unintended decisions on the part of the leading politicians and the military top brass of Europe was in fact inescapable behaviour. The great powers acted, in the words of Karl Marx, like a band of warring brothers; not just because they were committed to a system of competitive accumulation but because they were its prisoners and driven by its cold logic.

The rival imperialisms each tried to solve their own problems by expanding their territory, leading to collisions right across the world. Engels, quoted earlier, had read the writing on the wall as early as 1887.

Lions led by donkeys

"Lions led by donkeys" is the theme of Tory historian Alan Clark's influential book, *The Donkeys*, published in 1963. It concluded that most senior military officers were grossly

Empire and Revolution

incompetent and that "Haig in particular was an unhappy combination of ambition, obstinacy and megalomania".[9] And it was a thesis that caught the public mood.

Despite Tory minister Michael Gove's denunciation of "left-wing" historians (Alan Clark notwithstanding) and popular TV programmes like *Blackadder* for being unpatriotic, the verdict of popular culture is more or less unanimous:

> The First World War was stupid, tragic and futile. The stupidity of the war has been a theme of growing strength since the 1920s. From Robert Graves through "Oh, What a Lovely War!" to "Blackadder", the criminal idiocy of the British High Command has become an article of faith... The enormous success of Pat Barker's "Regeneration" trilogy testifies to the power of this view.[10]

As one ordinary foot soldier who survived the war wrote: "All officers above the rank of lieutenant-colonel should have been strangled at birth".[11] The experience of the class divide inside the armed forces was a powerful driver of anger. Lampooning the military top brass is preferable to rehabilitating them, which is precisely what the Tories are up to. For that reason alone Joan Littlewood's play, *Oh, What a Lovely War!* deserves a new audience. It is 50 years since it was first performed at the Theatre Royal Stratford, in London's East End. It showed the war through the eyes of the front line troops and those facing sacrifice at home. *Oh, What a Lovely War!* is an antidote to David Cameron's cynical claim that "we were all in it together then as now".

But simply denouncing the stupidity of the High Command and criticising the conduct of the war doesn't explain what caused it. Condemning millions to certain death was callous and brutal but not necessarily "stupid" from the standpoint of the ruling class. Would it have been acceptable if the war had been run more efficiently or more humanely? Or if the casualties had been lower?

Nonetheless, it is worth knowing how much Winston Churchill, First Lord of Admiralty, relished the First World War:

The British ultimatum to the Germans requesting an assurance on Belgian neutrality was set to expire at 11pm on 4 August. Half an hour beforehand Asquith sent a message to Lloyd George, asking him to join him in the Cabinet room. The Chancellor of the Exchequer found the Prime Minister sitting anxiously and later told Margot Asquith, "Big Ben struck eleven very slowly—we sat in complete silence for ten minutes after the last boom.

"Then the solemn atmosphere was shattered. Winston dashed into the room radiant, his face bright, his manner keen and he told us how he was going to send telegrams to the Mediterranean, the North Sea and God knows where! You could see he was a really happy man. I wondered if this was the state of mind to be in at the opening of such a fearful war as this." Nor was Lloyd George the only person who testified to this attitude of Churchill's. Violet Bonham-Carter recorded in her diary him saying in February 1915, "I love this war. I know it's smashing and shattering the lives of thousands every moment, and yet—I can't help it—I enjoy every second of it".[12]

The Churchill who so relished the First World War was the same warmonger who had been present during the butchery at Omdurman, sent the troops to shoot down striking Welsh miners in 1910, would send tanks into Glasgow in 1919 and order the RAF to use poison gas against the Kurdish rebels in British-ruled Iraq.

Imperialism—the highest stage of capitalism

No sane capitalist desires a war that kills 20 million, but sane or insane, every capitalist is part of an economic system bound up with military competition between nation states.

The generals and the politicians on all sides do bear responsibility. Some went to war gleefully, some with crocodile tears and some with real foreboding. But they all backed the war because they were acting in the interests of a class driven to perpetual competitive accumulation. That drive fuelled and directed the war.

Marx lived during the rise of industrial capitalism and developed the idea of "alienated labour"—explaining how the mass of producers become separated from the product of their labour; how that product takes on a life of its own and comes to dominate them; how the very labour of the worker creates the chains which tie him or her to endless production.

But it is not only the workers who become imprisoned in this process—the capitalist is trapped in it too, forced to compete in order to stay ahead of his or her rivals. This very competition undermines the health of the system overall, leading to periodic crises, which throw workers into poverty and cause unsuccessful firms to fail. What's good for one capitalist isn't necessarily good for the system.

Before and during the First World War, the Bolshevik leaders Lenin and Bukharin, as well as the Polish/German socialist Rosa Luxemburg, set about refining Marx's analysis of 19th century capitalism to better understand the rise of what they called monopoly capitalism. Their investigations helped explain the conflict between the great powers in a way which connected it to the economic system, enabling them to oppose the war more effectively.

They showed how the growth of capitalism led to military competition complementing and even replacing the economic competition for markets; they showed that in every capitalist country there was a concentration into fewer giant firms that were increasingly integrated into the state—what they called "state capitalist trusts"; and they showed that this growing scale of production could no longer be constrained within the boundaries of those states, forcing them to extend to new markets elsewhere. That meant annexing territories and establishing spheres of influence over others. It also meant enlarging armies and navies to safeguard markets, raw materials and production facilities that existed abroad. "The capitalists partition the world, not out of personal malice, but because the degree of concentration which has been reached forces them to adopt this method in order to get profits".[13]

But partition could only be agreed by *all* the competitors for a short period because, as some grew faster than others, the military balance between them would shift and the stronger ones would demand a bigger share of the world. Each state would act to protect and reinforce its economic and strategic interest at the expense of the others.

Lenin's pamphlet, *Imperialism: The Highest Stage of Capitalism* was written as a popular outline of the theory:

> Capitalism has grown into a world system of colonial oppression and financial strangulation of the overwhelming majority of the people of the world by a handful of "advanced" countries. And this "booty" is shared between two or three powerful world plunderers armed to the teeth (America, Great Britain, Japan), drawing the whole world into *their* war over the division of *their* booty.[14]

Lenin located the causes of the war in capitalism itself, showing how it was becoming as normal a capitalist mechanism as boom and slump: "Periods of peace can only be breathing spells between wars. Peaceful alliances prepare the way for wars, and in their turn grow out of wars".[15]

Bukharin spelled this out: "The anarchy of world capitalism—the opposition between social world labour and 'national' state appropriation—expresses itself in the collision of the states and in capitalist war. War is nothing other than the method of competition at a specific level of development".[16]

Empire and Revolution

Imperialism was no longer just about having colonies, although colonies remained important. It was now a world system in which no single capitalism could survive without trying to expand at the expense of the others—a system whose logic was militarisation and war.

2

When empires collide

In the 19th century industry spread rapidly across the globe and the first capitalist powers, Britain, France and Holland, were joined by new competitors—the US, Germany, Italy, Japan and Russia—in the battle for raw materials, cheap labour, world markets and spheres of influence.

Britain had been the dominant capitalist power, but by the end of the 19th century its star was fading and Germany and the US had caught up and begun to overtake. Although Britain was the most "capitalist" of the European powers, it was far from self-sufficient, relying heavily on cheap, imported food and raw materials.

By the time of the First World War the largest firms in the advanced capitalist countries depended on raw materials in one part of the world, production facilities in another and markets elsewhere. Preserving as much as possible of its privileged access to the non-European world was therefore a matter of life and death for the British ruling class. Superior sea power had been the foundation of Britannia's imperial strength. The navy protected all Britain's trade routes and could easily sever those of its competitors.

Challenged by Germany and others in the naval arms race that developed in the 1890s, Britain began to create a system of alliances that would soon lead to war.

While it seems ludicrous now, 1914 was hailed by British politicians as the "great war for civilisation", a noble cause to defend freedom. Some went even further—HG Wells called it "the war to end all wars". It turned out to be the exact opposite.

The human suffering was matched only by the massive profiteering by the rich. At the end of the war Britain's foreign secretary, Lord Curzon, admitted, "The Allies floated to victory on a wave of oil". This may explain how John D Rockefeller, owner of Standard Oil, became the world's first billionaire in 1916 and how the war gave birth to a fresh British Empire in the Middle East. At the start of the war Britain occupied Egypt and seized it from Turkey. By the end Britain had "acquired" several more oil producing territories and helped establish the Zionist colony in Palestine.

Dear little Belgium

The noble cause cited by Britain for declaring war on Germany in 1914 was "dear little Belgium". Belgium was presented as the unfortunate victim of aggressive German imperialism, largely on the basis that it looked like a tiny blob on the map of Europe. It was in fact a vicious colonial power in 1914, as anyone living in the Belgian Congo might confirm. In the 1880s King Leopold of Belgium had stolen this huge central African territory from its inhabitants and plundered its rich resources.

King Leopold's colonial regime was grisly and murderous, using methods notorious even by colonial standards. When the Congolese rebelled, his army destroyed their villages, raping and murdering the inhabitants. To prove that punitive action had been taken, the Belgian soldiers involved collected basket-loads of severed hands, hacked from their victims. They did so to prove they had not wasted ammunition and to claim bounty.[17]

Evidence of Leopold's brutality slowly emerged. By 1906 the entire population of the Congo faced extinction. The combination of famine, forced labour and genocide had wiped out millions. The population of the region fell from 20 million in 1891 to 8.5 million in 1911.

An international campaign against Leopold's private empire eventually forced the Belgian state to "nationalise" the colony in 1908, compensating their King to the tune of 110 million francs. Colonialism and exploitation of the Congo continued under the Belgian flag for the benefit of Belgian capital.[18]

The peak years of empire

Belgium was not alone. In 1870 most of Africa was still ruled by Africans; by 1914 the whole of sub-Saharan Africa had been carved up and partitioned into 23 separate colonial possessions owned by six of the European powers. Only the US puppet state of Liberia and the precariously independent Kingdom of Ethiopia survived.

In Asia the remaining independent states were either conquered like Burma or partitioned into spheres of influence by the great powers, as in the case of China. Such nominal independence as remained to states like Persia or Turkey was due entirely to the conflicts between their would-be conquerors; so too with Oceania and South America.

> These were the peak years of imperialism in ideology as well as in fact. The years of Rudyard Kipling's "white man's burden" and Cecil Rhodes' "I would annex the planets if I could". They were also the years in which European and US capitalism was undergoing profound, structural changes.
>
> Laissez-faire capitalism was giving way to monopoly capitalism... In 1904, in the US, John Moody cited 318 trusts, most of them formed after 1898, as evidence that control of business and capital was rapidly concentrating into fewer and fewer hands. Similarly, though in varying degrees, Marx's prediction that "one capitalist always kills many" was coming true with a vengeance.[19]

That these facts were connected with one another was the essential argument of Lenin's theory of imperialism: "Under

Empire and Revolution

modern capitalism, when monopolies prevail, the export of capital has become the typical feature".[20] The evidence for Lenin's case was impressive at the time. Britain was a good example, with foreign and colonial investments increasing at the rate of 74 percent per annum from 1883 to 1893.

The same tendency was present in all the imperialist countries in varying degrees. "The stability of late Victorian and Edwardian capitalism rested upon the export of capital. A way had been found of alleviating the inherent instability of the system—for a time and at a terrible price".[21]

No socialist agitator ever expressed the essence of imperialism better than US Major General Smedley D Butler:

> I spent 33 years and four months in active service as a member of our country's most agile military force—the Marine Corps. And during that period I spent most of my time as a high class muscle man for big business, for Wall Street and for the bankers. In short I was a racketeer for capitalism. Thus I helped make Mexico safe for American oil interests in 1914. I helped make Haiti and Cuba decent places for the National City Bank boys to collect revenues in. I helped purify Nicaragua for the international banking house of Brown Brothers between 1909 and 1912. I helped make Honduras "right" for the American fruit companies in 1903 and the Dominican Republic safe for American sugar interests in 1916. In China I helped see to it that Standard Oil went unmolested.[22]

The price of imperialism was paid by the exploited workers and peasants of the colonial world. It was also paid, contrary to Lenin's view, by the workers of the developed capitalist powers. Again, taking Britain as an example, real wages rose considerably until the mid-1890s. From 1896 to 1900 they held steady but between 1900 and 1913 real wages actually declined by 10 percent.[23]

It is very easy to misunderstand the classical Marxist

theories of imperialism since the very word has altered and its meaning expanded, as Anthony Brewer has explained:

> Today the word "imperialism" generally refers to the dominance of more developed over less developed countries. For classical Marxists it meant, primarily, rivalry between major capitalist countries, rivalry expressed in conflict over territory, taking political and military as well as economic forms, and leading ultimately to inter-imperialist war. The dominance of stronger countries over weaker is certainly implicit in this conception, but the focus is on the struggle for dominance, a struggle between the strongest in which less developed countries figure primarily as passive battle-grounds, not as active participants.[24]

This description fits entirely Europe in the run-up to the war. Long before 1914 Germany had overtaken Britain to become the world's second industrial power behind the US. It had the fastest industrial growth of all the European powers, allowing it to make enough concessions to a well-organised working class to ensure decades of social peace. But the success of German capitalism destabilised the international environment in which it operated.

Britain and France were weaker economically but each had a greater global presence. Germany had no empire and sections of German capital were demanding one. So Germany built battleships to challenge Britain's naval supremacy and Britain retaliated by building the "Dreadnoughts". Germany planned the Berlin-Baghdad railway to run down through south east Europe and Turkey to the Persian Gulf. Britain and France formed a military alliance with Russia against Germany and its allies—Austro-Hungary and Turkey. France increased its conscript army to match Germany's military might and Russia designed its railway system with a future war against Germany, Austro-Hungary and Turkey in mind.

The Balkan Wars and Serbian nationalism

That imperialism meant wars between colonial powers as well as the enslavement of colonial peoples had been shown as early as 1904, when Russia's drive to the Pacific collided with Japan's drive west. Russia's military defeat sparked the 1905 Russian Revolution. War between the great powers threatened again, in 1906 and 1911, with a clash of French and German interests in Morocco.

Rival imperialisms pushed and collided against each other's influence in North, East and Southern Africa and in the Middle East. But, as Chris Harman wrote:

> The truly dangerous area was south-east Europe—the Balkans, where the Great Powers regarded particular local states as clients. There had been wars between these states in 1912 and in 1913. First Serbia, Greece, Montenegro and Bulgaria fell upon the remaining Turkish territories of Thrace and Macedonia, leaving Turkey with only a narrow strip of Eastern Thrace. Then Greece, Serbia and Romania, egged on by the Great Powers, fell upon Bulgaria.[25]

Leon Trotsky was a war correspondent in the Balkans in 1912-13. On the eve of the First World War he reported on the terrible legacy left by Russia, France, Germany and Britain as they meddled in Balkan affairs and competed to expand and control access to important trade routes:

> The states that today occupy the Balkan Peninsula were manufactured by European diplomacy around the table at the Congress of Berlin in 1879. There it was that all the measures were taken to convert the national diversity of the region into a regular mêlée of petty states. None of them was to develop beyond a certain limit, each separately was entangled in diplomatic bonds, and counter posed to all the rest, and finally the whole lot were condemned to helplessness in

relation to the Great Powers and their continual intrigues and machinations.[26]

The first Balkan War of 1912 ended in the Treaty of London; the second Balkan War of 1913 ended in the Treaty of Bucharest. But Trotsky warned treaties could not remove the pressures leading to war:

> The new boundary lines have been drawn across the living bodies of nations that have been lacerated, bled white and exhausted. Every one of the Balkan states now includes within its borders a compact minority that is hostile to it. Such are the results of the work carried out by the capitalist governments.[27]

The whole region was an explosive powder keg. How explosive was shown in June 1914 when the heir to the Hapsburg dynasty, Archduke Franz Ferdinand, visited the Austrian-run province of Bosnia. He was assassinated in Sarajevo by Serbian nationalists who wanted to drive the Austrians out of the province and incorporate it into neighbouring Serbia.

What happened immediately thereafter is a matter of diplomatic record. Austria declared war on Serbia, Russia's client state; Russia declared war on Austria; Germany told Russia to stay out of the crisis; France backed Russia, its ally; Britain supported France and went to war against Germany, using the pretext of German troops moving through Belgium as the excuse.

Within weeks, 44 years of peace in Western Europe gave way to war involving all its major states.

The shooting of the Austrian Archduke by Gavrilo Princip was the spark but not the cause of the First World War. The economic and military competition between the rival European imperialisms had stoked up the pressure to such an extent that war was inevitable at some point. The

Empire and Revolution

rivalries and conflicts of the great robber powers exploded in the summer of 1914 into the greatest organised slaughter the world had yet seen. Tens of millions went out to fight for their masters and 20 million would die—half of them civilians. What Lenin dubbed "an epoch of wars and revolutions" had begun for real.

3

Struggle derailed?

The war had been preceded by a decade of strikes and popular movements. In 1905 the Russian Empire had seen mass strikes, the first appearance of workers' councils (soviets) and the first workers' revolution. The 1905 Revolution was defeated, but it inspired workers across the continent and prompted developments in Marxist theory, not least Rosa Luxemburg's pamphlet, *The Mass Strike*. In it she analysed how mass workers' movements could fuse economic and political questions into potentially revolutionary waves.

In 1907 the mass strike resurfaced on the Belfast waterfront. It was a strike of the poorest workers for decent wages and trade union rights. For the first time unskilled and previously unorganised Protestant and Catholic dock labourers fought side by side against their Unionist bosses and the state. The strike was led by the firebrand union organiser Jim Larkin and thousands flocked to the dock workers' union. Battleships were sent to Belfast Lough, troops attacked the pickets, killing three of them. The strain of protecting the scabs provoked a police strike and the entire city was thrown into chaos.

Big and bitter strikes like this swept North America and Europe right up until the outbreak of war. There were large strikes and marches by women sweatshop workers throughout Manhattan's Lower East Side. Working in factories described as the "vilest and foulest industrial sores of New York", they struck for union rights and the right to vote. This "Uprising of the 30,000" in 1909 involved mainly Russian Jewish teenagers and was led by the young

Jewish socialist Clara Lemlich. It was in their honour that the German socialist Clara Zetkin founded International Working Women's Day.

1911 brought the Mexican Revolution, led by Emiliano Zapata and Francisco "Pancho" Villa. 1912 saw the legendary "Bread and Roses" textile workers' strike in Lawrence, Massachusetts, where 20,000 workers from a dozen national backgrounds took on their bosses. Led by women and organised by the militant Industrial Workers of the World (IWW), the strike was victorious.

In 1911 metalworkers in Bilbao, Spain, launched a general strike, provoking a solidarity strike in Barcelona. The years between 1911 and 1914 saw big struggles in rapidly industrialising Italy. In 1911 there were strikes opposing Italy's conquest of Libya and in Turin engineering workers rose up in an unofficial strike against attacks on conditions that their trade union leaders had agreed. The strike was defeated after ten weeks but the following year a 13-week strike recouped some of the losses. A new feature here was the creation from below of rank and file bodies known as internal commissions. The commissions organised in the workplace regardless of union membership. They would become the building blocks of the workers' council movement that developed in Turin at the end of the war.

In June 1914 agitation against the coming war led to a massive revolt. The spark came when a demonstration in the port of Ancona was fired on by the police and three workers were killed. A general strike was called and insurrection spread throughout the region of Emilia-Romagna. Whole towns were taken over and the red flag flown above the town halls. Ancona's "Red Week" saw the town held by the rebels. It took 100,000 troops to suppress the resistance and isolate the Turin general strike.

Even in Germany, where the level of struggle was lower, there was a wave of strikes between 1910 and 1912 in favour of extending the franchise to more workers, which led to clashes with the police. There was also a bitter miners' strike in the Ruhr coalfield.

Britain before the war

In Britain the years before the First World War are often depicted as a golden age. Britain's empire covered the globe, the economy seemed strong and with Asquith's Liberal Party winning re-election in 1910, political stability seemed assured.

In 1910 the great movement for women's suffrage, led by the Women's Social & Political Union (WSPU) had been quietened. Certainly in the early years of the movement, the infectious spirit of militant defiance spread deep into the consciousness of women of all classes. But in 1910 its middle class leadership around Emmeline Pankhurst and her daughter Christabel agreed a temporary truce with the Liberals, in return for a promise of legislation.

In the 20 years since the wave of "new unionism" and the legendary docks strike of 1889, the official trade union movement had fallen asleep:

> The horizons of the trade union leaders were firmly limited by the Liberal Party, which most of them still supported, and the new but supine Labour Party... The advice passed on to militant demands from below was to "hold your fire". Pretty well everyone in the new Labour leadership agreed that strikes were a waste of time and effort and that time and effort should be devoted instead to Labour's advance in parliament.[28]

But something dramatic was about to happen. As the leaders of the WSPU maintained the truce and held back their angry suffragette army through 1910 and 1911, the most militant period in British working class history was set to explode. "Between 1910 and 1914 and against the wishes of

Empire and Revolution

their own leaders, British workers plunged into a series of furious strikes which, but for the declaration of war, would have culminated in September 1914, in a general strike of extraordinary violence".[29]

The causes of the Great Unrest, as it came to be called, are easy to identify. Trade union membership had trebled since 1889 but real wages fell between 1900 and 1912. "Everyone in society seemed to have gained in the glittering Edwardian era—except the workers".[30] Over the next four years a tidal wave of strikes engulfed the whole of mainland Britain and colonial Ireland. And this rising struggle coincided with the resurgence of militancy in the suffrage movement after 1912 and the threat of civil war over Irish Home Rule in 1914.

The Great Unrest centred on huge strikes—first in all the ports, then the railways and the mines. It began in Southampton, then spread into dozens of different industries the length and breadth of the UK. The movement involved unskilled and often non-unionised workers. And it directly involved large numbers of women workers.

Singers, an American company, opened the biggest sewing machine factory in the world at Clydebank in Scotland. It was at the forefront of managerial and technological innovation and employed over 12,000 workers in assembly line mass production. Most were unskilled and a third of them women. In 1911 a strike began when a group of women downed tools against a speed-up. Within days the whole factory was on strike.

Led by a group of young revolutionaries influenced by the IWW, the strike was eventually defeated and 300 activists victimised. But the "troublemakers" were dispersed around Clydeside engineering factories and would play a key role in the shop stewards' movement that developed at the start of the war.

Elsewhere the movement was on the up:

Old sectarian differences between workers, soured by centuries of prejudice, were swept aside. In Liverpool and Dublin orange and green banners joined the demonstrations. In South Wales the police went on strike. So did the schoolchildren—in 1911 alone there were 62 school strikes, most of them in South Wales.

Trade union membership in that single year grew by over 600,000 and the unions themselves were transformed. The old moderates had no stomach for these new battles. Where there were elections, as in the South Wales Miners' Federation, the veterans were replaced by eager young militants, hungry for action. The famous 1912 pamphlet, *The Miners' Next Step*, was the work of these tempestuous young leaders.[31]

The industrial unrest in the summer of 1911 centred on the London dock strike. It effectively brought the capital to a standstill. In August 1911 in Bermondsey hundreds of women at a sweet factory walked out after hearing that the national transport workers' strike had started.

They were immediately joined by other women and girls from all the other local workplaces—workers who were poorly paid and had never belonged to a trade union but decided it was time they did. Mary Macarthur, president of the National Federation of Women Workers, set up a local strike headquarters and women joined the union in droves. The strikers organised flying pickets to pull out other groups of workers. "In the East End and in South London, bottle washers, tin box makers, cocoa makers, distillery workers, rag pickers, 'sweated' and unorganised women and girls earning from five to ten shillings a week, emulated the action of the London transport workers and came out on strike".[32]

At one point 15,000 striking women cheered the transport union strike leaders at an enormous meeting in Southwark Park. A strike of London County Council cleaners won a minimum wage, holiday pay and direct employment. At Cradley Heath in the West Midlands, women employed as chain makers struck and doubled their wages.

Helping to organise strikes among young women mill-workers on Clydeside, Glasgow socialist John Maclean wrote at the end of 1911: "The times we are living in are so stirring and full of change that it is not impossible to believe that we are living in the rapids of revolution".[33]

In 1912 alone well over 40 million working days were "lost" due to strikes and Maclean wrote, "Never were the masses so pugnacious...never were they so class conscious. Fighting leads to new facts, a new theory and thence to revolution".[34] Unlike Maclean, most commentators assumed the storm would pass, but it raged on through 1913. One of the biggest and longest battles was in Ireland—the five month Dublin lock-out of transport and other workers in 1913.

In 1910 Larkin had formed the Irish Transport & General Workers Union and from then until the outbreak of war in 1914 a succession of strikes swept the country. The bitter Dublin Lockout won massive solidarity and sympathy action from British workers, with street collections in towns and cities throughout the UK. But the Dublin struggle was sold out by the British TUC and the strikers were starved back to work.

Radical suffragette Sylvia Pankhurst had spoken in support of the Dublin strikers at the solidarity rally organised for them in London's Albert Hall. For doing so she was expelled from the WSPU by her mother and sister. Sadly during the Great Unrest the leadership of the WSPU mentioned strikers usually only to denounce them.

The Great Unrest rolled on into 1914 and right up to the start of the First World War. Between 1911 and 1914 trade union membership had doubled.

Irish Home Rule and the Curragh Mutiny

The Conservative and Unionist Party, as it was then officially known, was in cahoots with the unionist bosses who controlled Ulster. Together, and with the connivance of the Army top brass, they threatened a loyalist mutiny to either derail the Liberal government or force it to drop its Irish Home Rule Bill.

Unionist feeling ran high in the officer corps of the British army, many of whom hailed from Protestant Anglo-Irish families with a strong stake in the union. They made it clear that if the army were called upon to enforce Home Rule it would refuse. In a notorious incident in March 1914, 53 British officers at the Curragh army camp in County Kildare proposed to resign rather than force the introduction of Home Rule against unionist resistance. After three days the Liberal government gave in, announcing that British troops would not be used in Ulster.

Director of Military Operations Henry Wilson was a supporter of this officers' rebellion:

> Wilson made less and less effort to mask his contempt for "Squiff" (as he called Asquith) and his "filthy cabinet". He did not shrink from using the Home Rule question to blackmail the prime minister into meeting unionist demands. In a memorandum presented to the Army Council to be put before the cabinet on 29 June 1914, Wilson and his colleagues argued that the army would need to deploy the entire British Expeditionary Force to Ireland if it were to impose Home Rule and restore order there.
>
> In other words: if the British government wished to impose Home Rule, it would have to renounce any military intervention in Europe for the foreseeable future; conversely, a continental military intervention would mean forgoing the introduction of Home Rule. This meant in turn that officers of unionist sympathies—which were

extremely widespread in an officer corps dominated by Protestant Anglo-Irish families—were inclined to see in a British continental intervention one possible means of postponing or preventing altogether the introduction of Home Rule. Nowhere else in Europe, with the possible exception of Austria-Hungary, did domestic conditions exert such direct pressure on the political outlook of the most senior military commanders.[35]

This was dynamite. The British High Command were quite prepared to use the prospect of a European war as a way of defeating Home Rule for Ireland and were quite prepared to defy parliament to force the issue.

The outbreak of war allowed the ruling class to postpone Irish Home Rule on the basis of a terrible deal with the constitutional Irish Home Rule party, which meant that Ireland would be partitioned after the war with Ulster remaining in the UK.

The war also brought the Great Unrest to a juddering halt. Between January and July 9 million days had been lost to strikes, but from August to December 1914 only a million days were lost. Mobilisation for war in Europe seemed to have derailed the militancy across the continent, and in August 1914 opposition to the war became very difficult. How could this happen and what did it mean for internationalism?

4

The collapse of official socialism

"If war is declared, the working classes in the countries affected, as well as their parliamentary representatives, have the duty to mobilise their forces to prevent hostilities breaking out... If, in spite of their efforts, war should break out, their duty is to struggle actively for a speedy end to the fighting and make every effort to use the economic and political crisis, which the war causes, to rouse the people and hasten the abolition of the rule of the capitalist class."

—*Resolution of the Stuttgart Congress of the Second International, 1907, unanimously re-affirmed at its Basle Congress in 1912*[36]

In the run-up to war all the main labour and socialist parties, grouped together in the Second International, had re-affirmed their opposition to imperialist war. Yet on 4 August when war broke out, it shattered the international socialist movement.

Although it was an imperialist war—a war for colonies, markets and profit—the vast majority of the leaders of these Second International parties in nearly all the warring states abandoned internationalism and all their brave words of 1912; instead they chose national unity and backed their own governments.

There were a few brave exceptions. The Russian socialists, particularly the Bolsheviks, refused to support the Tsar's war machine. The Serbian party and the Bulgarian majority party stood their ground too, in the face of murderous persecution. The Italian and American socialist parties were not forced to choose immediately as their ruling classes remained neutral at the start, while the Spanish, Scandinavian and Dutch remained in this position throughout the war.

Everywhere else the socialists who openly opposed the war were at first a small minority; Rosa Luxemburg, Clara Zetkin, Franz Mehring and Karl Liebknecht in Germany; John Maclean and Sylvia Pankhurst in Britain; Alfred Rosmer in France; and James Connolly in Ireland.

From opposition to capitulation

The German Social Democratic Party (SPD) was the biggest and most influential socialist party in the Second International and claimed the heritage of Marx and Engels. On the eve of war it had 111 elected deputies in the Reichstag (the German parliament). Socialists everywhere looked to it for a lead.

On 20 February 1914, Rosa Luxemburg, leader of the SPD left wing and mover of the anti-war resolution at the 1907 International Congress in Stuttgart, was arrested for inciting soldiers to mutiny. The basis of the charge was a public speech in which she argued: "If they expect us to murder our French or other foreign brothers, then let us tell them, 'No, under no circumstances'."[37]

In court she turned defence into attack and her speech, published under the title *Militarism, War and the Working Class*, is one of the sharpest condemnations of imperialism. She was sentenced to a year in jail but not detained on the spot. On leaving the court she went straight to a demonstration and repeated almost word for word the same anti-war message. On 25 July an emergency edition of the SPD newspaper carried the leadership's appeal for mass demonstrations to stop the war:

> The class conscious German proletariat raises a fiery protest in the name of humanity and civilisation, against the

criminal activities of the war-mongers. Not a drop of a German soldier's blood must be sacrificed to the Austrian despots' lust for power. Comrades, we call on you to express in mass meetings the unshakeable will for peace.[38]

On Tuesday 28 July workers went onto the streets all over Germany. The next day the newspapers reported that very big demonstrations had taken place in all the cities and the larger towns—especially in the industrial areas. The same night thousands packed into Brussels' biggest meeting hall for an anti-war rally. They cheered as French socialist leader Jean Jaurès put his arm around Hugo Haase, the SPD parliamentary deputy.

Two days earlier in Paris the CGT union newspaper ran the headline, "Workers must answer any declaration of war by a revolutionary general strike" and the following day there was a massive anti-war march in Paris.[39] On 30 July the SPD paper *Vorwärts* declared: "The socialist proletariat refuses all responsibility for the events being conjured up by a ruling class blinded to the point of madness".[40]

On 31 July the International Socialist Bureau of the Second International issued its call for a struggle against war. The following day the German government declared war on Russia and proclaimed a state of emergency. That same day Jean Jaurès was assassinated on his return to Paris.

Two days later, on 3 August, the parliamentary group of the SPD decided it would vote in favour of war credits to finance the Kaiser's armies. Of their 111 deputies only 15 were prepared to vote against war but when their request to be allowed to do so was voted down, they submitted to party discipline. On 4 August the SPD parliamentary group of deputies trooped into the Reichstag and voted en-bloc to fund the war aims of the German government.

The party then issued the following statement, a complete about-turn from its anti-war stance issued days earlier:

For our people and its peace, much, if not everything, is at stake in the event of the victory of Russian despotism. Our task is to ward off the danger, to safeguard the culture and the independence of our own country. We do not leave the fatherland in the lurch in the hour of danger.[41]

The shock of betrayal

For Lenin, exiled from Russia, the outbreak of war was not unexpected. What shook him was the SPD's U-turn. When he read in *Vorwärts* the report of the Reichstag vote, he assumed the paper was a forgery, published by the German High Command to demoralise the opponents of the war. He was not the only socialist leader deeply shocked.

For Rosa Luxemburg it was a terrible blow but she overcame her immediate feeling of despair. On the same day the SPD deputies capitulated, a small group of socialists met in her Berlin apartment to organise against the war and mount a fight within their own party. It was not until November that Karl Liebknecht, one of the 15 SPD deputies opposed to war, defied party discipline to vote with his conscience in the Reichstag against further war credits. He joined the group around Rosa that would form the Spartacus League.

Trotsky, another exiled Russian socialist, remembers: "The telegram telling of the capitulation of German Social Democracy shocked me even more than the declaration of war in spite of the fact that I was far from a naïve idealising of German socialism".[42] Bukharin wrote that the vote on 4 August "was the greatest tragedy of our lives".[43]

Lenin was quick to come to terms with the truth. In July, weeks before the outbreak of war, he had written an article arguing for revolutionary opposition to war and it was no surprise that the Bolsheviks were the first to take a clear position on the 4 August debacle.

On 24 August Lenin drafted *The Tasks of Revolutionary Social Democracy in the European War*, which laid out a clear path for revolutionaries in the tough years that lay ahead. He was in no doubt about the "bourgeois, imperialist and dynastic" character of the war, or that the SPD vote was:

a betrayal of socialism. The leaders of the International committed treachery by voting for war credits, by justifying and defending the war and by joining the bourgeois governments of the belligerent countries... The responsibility for disgracing socialism falls primarily on the German social democrats, who were the strongest and most influential party in the Second International.[44]

The task of the working class was to fight the imperialist war by using the weapon of class struggle, culminating in civil war. In this Lenin was unequivocal. Revolutionary defeatism means welcoming the defeat of your own country: "The socialists of all belligerent countries should express their wish that all their 'own' governments should be defeated".[45]

Even though Lenin was for the defeat of his own ruling class, this did not imply that he considered the German ruling class any less bloodthirsty or imperialist. For him the war was not produced by the crimes of one country but by the general crisis of monopoly capitalism that could only be ended by revolution.

Class or nation?

When it came to the crunch the leaders of German socialism were terrified of being accused of betraying Germany. The Kaiser had taunted them as "fellows without a country". On 4 August they had decided not to "leave the fatherland in the lurch in its hour of danger", and betrayed the international working class instead.

The majority of the Social Democrat leaders in the Second International followed the SPD and backed the war. Emile Vandervelde, the executive secretary of the Second

International, entered his country's war cabinet. How could they justify such a betrayal to their own followers? By pointing to the evils of the enemy regimes. The excuse was that the enemy abroad was worse than the enemy at home.

To cover their betrayal, the SPD leaders argued Germany was a more progressive society than backward Russia. They told German workers that by fighting reactionary Tsarism and British colonialism the Kaiser's army was defending the prospects of socialism and its future victory in Europe. In the name of socialism they sent millions of young men to their deaths.

The Russian socialists who supported the war claimed they were fighting despotic Prussian militarism. In France the leaders of the Socialist Party and the syndicalist leaders of the CGT, the main union federation, swung behind their country's war effort, claiming they had no option but to enter a "sacred union" to defend their own country because the SPD had voted for the Kaiser's war budget. They argued German imperialism had to be destroyed if the possibility of socialism was to be assured.

The leaders of the British labour movement

In Britain the Labour Party and the trade union leaders backed the war as "a war for democracy"—despite the fact that they were fighting in alliance with autocratic, Tsarist Russia. Labour leader Ramsay MacDonald was a pacifist and when he voiced doubts about the conflict he was deposed by the patriotic trade union bureaucracy and replaced by Arthur Henderson.

In 1915 Henderson was rewarded with a cabinet post in the coalition National Government and through him Labour gave great assistance to the war effort. It was Henderson who arranged the 1915 Treasury Agreement, by which the unions abandoned many of their defences, including the right to strike. Speaking for the union leaders who now controlled the Labour Party, dockers' leader Ben Tillett championed patriotism and spoke at army recruitment rallies: "In a strike I am for my class, right or wrong; in a war I am for my country, right or wrong".[46]

Ludicrous though it seems, the "Marxist" leader of the British Socialist Party (BSP), H M Hyndman, had been calling for a bigger navy and an increased arms budget ever since 1910. Like the Labour and trade union leaders, he spoke on recruiting platforms, arguing that a defensive war against Germany in support of Belgium's freedom was justified.

His decision to throw the weight of the BSP into the government's recruiting drive produced a storm of protest from local branches. "One after another branches at Stepney, West Ham, Bow & Bromley, Central Hackney, Pollokshaws and elsewhere expressed their opposition. 15 of 18 London branches assembled at an all London Conference and demanded that the statement be withdrawn".[47]

Meanwhile in Glasgow John Maclean had already opposed the BSP leadership's line and won the local branches to an anti-war position:

> It is our business as socialists to develop "class patriotism", refusing to murder one another for a sordid world capitalism. The absurdity of the present situation is surely apparent when we see British socialists going out to murder German socialists with the object of crushing Kaiserism and Prussian militarism. The only real enemy to Kaiserism and Prussian militarism was and is German Social Democracy.[48]

Maclean launched his Glasgow-based paper, *The Vanguard*. It provided the first anti-war, anti-Hyndman opposition within the party and set the pace for a movement, which would eventually break the power of the old guard who ran the BSP.

Lenin was quick to expose the hypocrisy of all the European ruling classes: "The bourgeoisie of each country is asserting that it is out to defeat the enemy—not for plunder and the seizure of territory but for the liberation of all other peoples except its own." He also castigated the official leaders of the working class movement for tailing behind their own ruling classes and for lying to themselves and their followers about the nature of the war:

> It seems only yesterday that Hyndman, having turned to the defence of imperialism prior to the war, was looked upon by all decent socialists as an unbalanced crank and that nobody spoke of him otherwise than in a tone of disdain. Now the most eminent Social Democrat leaders of all the countries have sunk to Hyndman's position.[49]

The illusion of the "peaceful road" to socialism

The Second International died on 4 August 1914, but its death was not quite as sudden as it then seemed. With hindsight it is easy to see that the vote for war by the SPD in the Reichstag did not come out of the blue but was the culmination of years of adapting to imperialism and parliamentary politics. While the leaders of the Second International talked class struggle and Marxism at May Day rallies, their day-to-day practice was strictly reformist. The prospect of a peaceful road to socialism had seemed to open up; instead it led to the slaughter of 1914.

The Second International had been founded at a special congress in Paris on 14 July 1889—the centenary of the storming of the Bastille and the outbreak of the French Revolution. It proclaimed itself heir to the First International in which Karl Marx himself played a leading role. Launched with what looked to be revolutionary intent, the International became the focus for some flourishing workers' parties, which commonly called themselves social democratic—a term Marx disliked, preferring "communist".

They were not the only workers' parties but they grew to

dominate the movement in the years up to 1914. The rapid expansion of industry and the growth of the working class created a new, mass audience for these socialist organisations in the late 19th century. But following the defeat of Chartism in Britain, the failure of the European revolutions of 1848 and the crushing of the Paris Commune in 1871, their leaders did not feel confident to directly challenge the state.

Instead they followed a strategy developed by socialists in Germany, which took advantage of limited electoral reforms to win votes and seats in local councils and national parliaments. Alongside this electoral approach and subordinate to it, they focussed on building the trade unions and other forms of working class organisation like co-operatives, sports and cultural clubs. The German party was the model for others. It was founded in 1875 and operated in conditions of illegality until 1890, but by 1912 it was polling 4.25 million votes and had over 100 deputies elected to the Reichstag. In 1914 it had well over a million members.

In France the United Socialist Party (SFIO) was founded in 1905 and won 102 seats in the election held in early 1914. The year before the Italian Socialist Party (PSI) won a quarter of the total votes cast and 78 deputies. The Austro-Hungarian party had won over a million votes and 82 deputies. In the US the American Socialist Party, founded in 1901, had by 1912 gained 125,000 members and polled 800,000 votes. Parties on this model were built in Poland, Sweden, Belgium and the Netherlands. In Britain success for the left was much more modest but nonetheless real; in the 1906 general election the newly formed Labour Party returned 29 MPs.

As Duncan Hallas explained:

From Scandinavia to the Balkans "Marxist" social democratic parties gained members, votes and deputies... Weaker but nonetheless significant movements were developing from Britain and Chile to Spain, Switzerland and Uruguay, all of them affiliated to the Second International and apparently committed to the socialist reconstruction of society and an uncompromising opposition to "national unity" and war... It was an illusion.

There were differences between the various parties but basically they were pseudo revolutionary, combining an uncompromising verbal hostility to capitalism with a practical activity that was confined to winning members and votes (the British and Australian Labour Parties were exceptional in lacking Marxist rhetoric and revolutionary pretensions).[50]

Karl Kautsky, theoretician of the SPD and the International was regarded as "the Pope of Marxism". He had long argued that the downfall of capitalism was inevitable. Socialists could patiently wait for it to happen. Yet this mechanical, "do nothing" Marxism was a complete negation of Marx's insistence on the centrality of class struggle and working class self-activity. "This impressive apparatus had become an end in itself. Confrontation with the state, or even the employers, was avoided where possible. As a political force social democracy was passive".[51] The priority of the SPD—and most other social democratic and labour parties that took their lead from it—was to patiently convince the workers to vote socialist in elections.

Though the German trade unions were strong they were seen as having an auxiliary and subsidiary role—"the economic struggle"—as outlined in the party's programme.

By 1913 the SPD and its trade unions owned property worth 90 million marks. The party had a layer of parliamentarians, trade union bureaucrats and full time workers. Having painstakingly built up a stake in bourgeoisie society, the SPD leaders were scared of losing it. They had a lot more to lose than their chains.

August 1914 exposed the truth. The combination of verbal radicalism and political passivity was no longer possible to sustain mass parties in the nation states that were going to war. The party leaders had to choose: maintain their internationalism, oppose the war, face imprisonment and the seizure of their assets; or support their own state.

Opposition to the war

There were groups of workers ready to resist the jingoism and war fever. Socialists and trade union militants were used to lies in the press and their principles coming under attack. The Great Unrest had seen a doubling of trade union membership and the emergence of a wide range of socialist groups which rejected the parliamentary road and stressed direct action. These groups had campaigned against the war in the run-up to it. In the days before hostilities broke out there were mass demonstrations of workers against war throughout Europe. Thousands flocked to rallies in London, Paris, Brussels, Berlin and St Petersburg on the eve of war to hear and cheer their leaders calling for peace. The huge rallies organised by the SPD had so scared the Kaiser that he considered proclaiming martial law to have the SPD leadership arrested.

As late as August 1914 even the official leadership of the British Labour Party was involved in the anti-war agitation and participated in the monster anti-war rally in Trafalgar Square, where Keir Hardie and Arthur Henderson demanded: "Workers stand together for peace! Combine and conquer the militarist enemy and the self-seeking imperialists today, once and for all... Down with class rule! Down with the rule of brute force! Down with the war!"[52]

But once war was declared, those same leaders rushed to support it. The German and Austrian Social Democratic parties, the British Labour Party, the TUC and the leaders of the British Socialist Party, French socialist and trade

Empire and Revolution

union leaders, the veteran Russian Marxist Plekhanov and the anarchist Kropotkin—all backed their own rulers.

Those who had doubts—Hugo Haase and Karl Kautsky in Germany or Keir Hardie, Philip Snowden and Ramsay MacDonald in Britain, fudged or kept quiet in order to preserve party unity and avoid being accused of betraying the nation.

Keir Hardie opposed the war on pacifist grounds and had even suggested that the threat of a European General Strike could prevent it. Yet only a few days after it started he wrote, "A nation at war must be united. With the boom of the enemy's guns within earshot, the boys who have gone forth to fight their country's battles must not be disheartened by any discordant note at home." At the end of 1915 he wrote, "I have never said or written anything to dissuade young men from enlisting".[53]

It was not the lack of a movement which resulted in cowardice on the part of the socialist and trade union leaders; rather it was the cowardice of the leaders that demobilised the movement as it faced its greatest test. There is no denying the growing pro-war mood at the point when war broke out, but as the existence of a widespread anti-war movement before the war—and the mounting opposition as it went on—showed, the basis for resistance always existed. In the week that the war began, James Connolly expressed his anger and frustration in the Glasgow-based socialist newspaper, *Forward*:

> What then becomes of all our resolutions, all our protests of fraternisation, all our threats of general strikes...all our hopes for the future? Were they all as sound and fury, signifying nothing? Even an unsuccessful attempt at social revolution by force of arms would be less disastrous to the socialist cause than the act of socialists allowing themselves to be used in the slaughter of their brothers in the cause. A

great continental uprising of the working class would stop the war: a universal protest at public meetings will not save a single life from being wantonly slaughtered.[54]

Having voted for war the SPD leaders were admitted to the inner circle around the Kaiser's government, where they stayed for four years, increasingly isolated from German workers and losing any feel for the mood among them and the soldiers at the front. If instead the leaders of the SPD and the other European socialist and labour parties had stood by their principles, like the Russians and Serbians, they could have shortened or even stopped the bloodbath to come. Harry McShane, a Clydeside shop steward who opposed the war from the start, described the dire situation on the left:

Even although we didn't expect just how terrible the war was going to be, we knew it was a political disaster. Our hopes for an international general strike to stop the war were unfounded. Every section of the International supported its own country's war efforts. Only a few revolutionaries stood out—Lenin's Bolsheviks in Russia, Rosa Luxemburg and Karl Liebknecht in Germany.

In Britain the socialist movement was split over the war. Many socialists were pacifists. In the ILP [Independent Labour Party] there was a good deal of anti-war feeling but the leaders took a very weak stand and the national policy was not clear. In February 1915 Keir Hardie presided over a meeting in London of socialist parties from the allied countries that actually declared in favour of an allied victory.[55]

The executive of the BSP urged its membership to actively support the war effort. The majority of the members opposed this decision and the London and Glasgow branches met and rejected it overwhelmingly. But a majority of the opposition were themselves confused, adopting either a pacifist approach or arguing for "defencism", whereby war could

Empire and Revolution

be supported in so far as it was a defence against German aggression but not for territorial advantage.

The international labour movement was now split into three main tendencies: the reformist right wing, outright supporters of the war; the centre, led by Karl Kautsky, who sought to achieve peace within the framework of capitalism; and the revolutionary left—Lenin and the Bolsheviks, the group around Rosa Luxemburg and Karl Liebknecht and various other individual socialists such as John Maclean, James Connolly and Alfred Rosmer—for whom only socialist revolution could put an end to war.

From his Swiss exile Lenin issued a stream of statements and pamphlets, from "The Tasks of Revolutionary Social Democracy in the European War" written in August 1914 through to "Socialism and War", written jointly with Zinoviev in July 1915. He had a clear idea of what must be done: "The so-called Centre of the German and other Social-Democratic parties has in actual fact faint-heartedly capitulated to the opportunists. A new, Third International must be built on the basis of uncompromising internationalism".[56]

5

Propaganda and class consciousness

"People were excited; they weren't horrified by it as they were in the Second World War—it was completely different. They rushed out in the street, followed the soldiers as they marched and kissed them, threw flowers and seemed to think it was something to be thrilled about because we were told it was all going to be over by Christmas... We were conned. We were made to believe this was a war to end all wars and there'd never be another one".[57]

At first the war was popular. In Britain Kitchener's appeal for volunteers saw 750,000 enlist in the first months.[58] Willie Gallacher was a revolutionary shop steward, who led the Clyde Workers' Committee from 1915 and was a founder member of the Communist Party in 1920. His book, *Revolt on the Clyde*, recalls the initial enthusiasm for war among some of his own class:

What a terrible attraction a war can be! The wild excitement, the illusion of wonderful adventure and the actual break in the deadly monotony of working class life! Thousands went flocking to the colours in the first days, not because of any "love of country", not because of any high feeling of "patriotism" but because of the new, strange and thrilling life that lay before them. Later the reality of the fearsome slaughterhouse, with all its long agony of filth and horror, turned them from buoyant youth to despair or madness.[59]

My own grandfather lied about his age, enlisted and ran away to war as a 14 year old to avoid going down the pit like his father and his older brother. He was wounded at Ypres at the end of 1914 and the experience helped make him a socialist.

Trotsky, exiled from Russia since his escape from Siberia in 1907, reacted to the enthusiasm on the streets of Vienna in much the same way as Willie Gallacher, explaining the pro-war mood more as a reaction to people's humdrum lives than to any deep-seated nationalism:

> The people whose lives, day in day out, pass in the monotony of hopelessness are many; they are the mainstay of modern society. The alarm of mobilisation brings into their lives a promise; the familiar and long hated is overthrown and the new and unusual reigns in its place. Changes still more incredible are in store for them in the future. For better or worse? For better, of course—what can seem worse than "normal" conditions? War affects everybody and those who are oppressed and deceived by life consequently feel that they are on an equal footing with the rich and powerful.[60]

Victor Serge, the Belgian socialist imprisoned in Paris when war was declared, described how, "Passionate singing of the Marseillaise, from crowds seeing off troops to the train, drifted across even to our jail. We could hear shouts of 'To Berlin! To Berlin!'"[61]

Most of the time, the prevailing ideas in society are the ideas of the ruling class.

> The determination of Europe's ruling classes to go to war with one another in 1914 was transmitted in a thousand ways to the middle classes and sections of the working class—through patriotic speeches and newspaper stories about "enemy atrocities", through marching bands and popular songs, and through declarations by novelists, poets and

philosophers. Schoolteachers repeated this to adolescent boys urging them to go and fight. Anyone who dissented was guilty of "stabbing our boys in the back".[62]

In Britain white feathers—a supposed symbol of cowardice—were publicly handed out by women to young men who had not enlisted. Jingoism was deliberately manufactured but the pressure it created was real. Anti-German hysteria was whipped up by the government and the press, but some prominent union leaders were at it too. Harry McShane recalls:

> Ben Tillett toured the country telling how he had seen a greasy spot on a wall where a German had bashed a baby's brains out. He poured out atrocity stories against the Germans and became hateful, really damn well hateful. And there were others who did the same.[63]

Such vile propaganda meant that at the start of the war German shops were attacked and many families with German or German-sounding names changed them.

Patriotism and the working class

Conventional accounts of the early war years often claim that all the warring states were swept by a patriotic frenzy and mass enthusiasm for war. While it would be wrong to deny that jingoism affected considerable sections of the population, including large sections of the working class, it is also wrong to suggest that it dominated the entire working class.

In May 1915, when it became clear that the Italian ruling class wanted to enter the conflict, there was an anti-war general strike in the working class citadel of Turin.

Even right at the start, the popularity of the war was not as widespread or deeply ingrained in the mass of ordinary people as the pro-war demonstrations, the singing of

Empire and Revolution

patriotic songs and the mass volunteering seemed to suggest. Writing about the alleged war hysteria in Germany, historian David Blackbourn points out: "The patriotic demonstrations of late July involved relatively small groups, with students and young salesmen prominent. Working class areas like the Ruhr were quiet".[64]

Alexander Shlyapnikov, an engineering worker in St Petersburg, noted this too. In his memoirs he contrasted the enthusiasm for war in August 1914 among the middle and upper classes with the more subdued mood in the factories:

The St Petersburg press did much to kindle popular chauvinism. They skilfully blew up "German" atrocities against Russian women and old men living in Germany. But even this hostile atmosphere did not drive workers to an excess of nationalism...one could not conclude that the Russian workers hated the Germans, as the newspapers claimed. This "literary chauvinism" considerably outweighed the actual mood even of the petty-bourgeois circles".[65]

Shlyapnikov's point was confirmed by events; on the day the Russian army was mobilised, 20 factories in St Petersburg struck in opposition to the war.

Manufacturing jingoism

Similarly in Britain patriotism and a desire to go to war did not arise spontaneously. Some people were jingoistic and many were susceptible to jingoism, especially at the start of the war, but enthusiasm and war fervour had to be manufactured and cranked up, as Ian Birchall has described:

Those who argue that jingoism penetrated the great mass of workers have as their most fundamental argument the fact that a million workers did volunteer before the supply was exhausted and conscription was introduced in 1916... The British ruling class got their volunteers but they had to work at it. Public sensibility was inflamed by numerous unsubstantiated atrocity stories.

In September 1914 the *Dumfries Standard* carried a story, soon prominently taken up by such London papers as *The Globe*, *The Star* and *The Evening Standard*, of a British nurse in Belgium who was said to have had both breasts cut off by German soldiers. In fact the nurse in question had never been in Belgium and the story had been invented by her younger sister.[66]

Fully aware of the importance of propaganda the cabinet appointed Charles Masterman as their spin doctor. In September 1914 Masterman organised a meeting of prominent writers who backed the war, including Thomas Hardy, H G Wells, Arnold Bennett, Arthur Conan Doyle, John Buchan and others. A considerable amount of patriotic prose and verse was churned out to justify the war and Britain's "destiny and duty". Buchan, a devoted imperialist and author of the best-selling, anti-German spy story, *The Thirty Nine Steps*, became the government's Director of Information. The war lobby produced propaganda films, including *Battle of the Somme*, seen by 19 million people in six weeks.

The WSPU also backed the war and colluded with the government. Its leaders had always insisted that the question of the vote should predominate over every other issue. Now the vote was tossed aside as Emmeline and Christabel Pankhurst declared that the supreme priority was winning the war. They toured the country demanding young men should enlist and helped initiate the practice of handing out white feathers. In early 1915 when engineering workers in Glasgow and miners in South Wales dared to go on strike the WPSU leaders denounced them as traitors. Paul Foot writes:

As they both confessed—even boasted—what was left of the WSPU played little part in the few moves that were made

to maintain the pre-war momentum for votes for women...
It was left chiefly to the anti-war minority of women,
represented by Sylvia Pankhurst and the more militant suffragettes, to raise the old slogans.[67]

Helen Crawfurd was one of those militant suffragettes.
Before the war she had been imprisoned on three occasions
and held under Asquith's notorious "Cat and Mouse Act",
whereby hunger-striking suffragettes were released as soon as
they became ill only to be re-imprisoned on the same charges
once they were well. Like Sylvia Pankhurst she was prominent in her opposition to the war and supported the strikes.
She broke with the WSPU in 1914 because of its pro-war
stance and in 1915 she led the Glasgow Women's Housing
Association, rallying working class housewives behind the
Glasgow rent strike.

In April 1915 the WSPU periodical, *The Suffragette*,
changed its name to *Britannia* and held a pro-war rally in
London in July. Emmeline Pankhurst organised a "Right
to Serve" demonstration demanding women should be able
to fight. It was backed by Lloyd George and funded by the
Treasury.

Emmeline Pankhurst had been in prison for inciting the
blowing up of Lloyd George's house but now both were smil-
ing as they appeared together before the cheering crowd. For
months afterwards newspapers celebrated the odd new cou-
ple. As one headline put it, "The Ablest Woman, The Ablest
Man in England. Once They Were Enemies, War Has Made
Them Friends".[68]

When a peace conference was called in the Hague in 1915,
Emmeline agitated against it and got the government to can-
cel the boat service from Tilbury so delegates could not attend.
Her support for the war was unrelenting. In February 1917
she travelled to Russia to support its provisional government

against the workers and soldiers who were demanding peace.

While the WSPU aided the British government, the pro-war stand taken by the Labour and trade union leaders was much more important. Arthur Henderson, who replaced pacifist Ramsay MacDonald as Labour leader, chaired the Peace Emergency Committee, which had representatives from the Labour Party and the TUC. The day after war was declared he changed its name to the War Emergency Committee and was instrumental in getting the union leaders to curtail strikes. In all the combatant countries the labour leaders were incorporated into the state machine because the bosses and politicians knew they were indispensable in mobilising their members behind the war.

Yet despite all the propaganda and coercion, even at the beginning of the war large numbers of ordinary people were not fooled by it:

> Those of us who are sometimes distressed by the fact that football seems to mobilise so much more energy than politics may be consoled by the thought that it cuts both ways as is shown by this observation from the diary of a Times journalist at the Chelsea football ground for the game against Arsenal in December 1914:
>
> "The posters carried by a line of sandwich men walking up and down before the gates of the Chelsea football ground declaimed: 'Are you Forgetting there is a War on?', 'Your Country Needs You', 'Be ready to Defend your Home and Women from the German Huns'. So far as I could see little attention was given to these skeletons at the feast".
>
> Such varied expressions of a sullen and blinkered apathy are a long way removed from proletarian internationalism, but they do show clearly that "patriotic frenzy" had not penetrated the working class so deeply as is often believed.[69]

Today Michael Gove claims most went to war willingly because they were fighting for democracy. He is wrong. The volunteers dried up and conscription had to be introduced in 1916. The large number of early volunteers requires careful scrutiny; no doubt many did enlist out of patriotism, while others volunteered because they were told the war would be over by Christmas. But many enlisted to escape economic hardship and unemployment. A pamphlet produced by the National Service League entitled, "The Briton's First Duty", conceded: "Want and hunger are, unfortunately for us, the invisible recruiting sergeants of a great portion of our army".[70]

Many "volunteers" were pressured by their employers:

[They were] the victims of intimidation, which went far beyond peer pressure and young ladies with white feathers. Thus when 7,000 London tram workers struck for 19 days in May 1915, the reaction of their London County Council bosses was to sack all the men of military age, telling them to volunteer for the armed forces.[71]

In November 1915 the press reported, "The Prime Minister's declaration that all unmarried men must serve their country has had a stimulating effect in the City... In many of the large city offices and warehouses a census has been taken of the eligibles, who are being asked to give their employers reasons for not enlisting". At the outbreak of war, the Prince of Wales Fund, ostensibly a charity to relieve distress resulting from the conflict, "was frequently administered by those who were sometimes not above instituting, in relation to able-bodied men of military age, their own local system of compulsory military service sanctioned by the threat of starvation".[72]

Control, coercion and conscription
The working class had to be controlled and coerced as well as convinced. Anti-war socialists and pacifists were censored, hounded and jailed. Draconian sentences were meted

out to deter any opposition and resistance. In Derby a family of anti-war activists were framed and charged with plotting to assassinate Lloyd George. The mother, Alice Wheeldon, was sentenced to ten years' hard labour. Other members of the family served prison sentences too. When the Hague Women's Peace Conference was held in 1915 the British women who wanted to attend were denied passports by the government.

In March 1916, when conscription into the armed forces was finally introduced, John Maclean warned: "Conscription means the bringing of all young men under the control of the military authorities—whether they be in the field of battle or in the factory or workshop".[73] There was mass opposition to conscription including mass strikes in engineering, as well as widespread draft-dodging.

MacLean was sacked for his anti-war activities and jailed on three separate occasions during the war for treason and sedition. Each time he was released because of mass working class protest. The leaders of the Clyde Workers' Committee were all either arrested or deported from Glasgow during 1916 for leading resistance to the war economy. Maclean's newspaper, *The Vanguard*, the Glasgow ILP newspaper, *Forward*, and the Clyde Workers' Committee paper, *The Worker*, were all shut down by the state and Maclean's printing press was smashed.

By the end of 1917 the government was employing over 4,000 censors and hundreds of spies and agents provocateur to operate against trade union and anti-war activists. Legislation was used to prevent strikes and to stop workers changing jobs.

The use of force was greatest in the army and at the front. Six thousand conscientious objectors were imprisoned and 80 died in jail. Over 300 British soldiers were executed and thousands were jailed for desertion, insubordination and mutiny.

Empire and Revolution

The same things were happening in all the countries at war. In Germany workers who openly opposed the war or agitated for strikes were conscripted to the front. Rosa Luxemburg was imprisoned in February 1915 and remained incarcerated for most of the war with only brief spells of freedom. In 1916 Karl Liebknecht was sentenced to two and a half years hard labour for his May Day speech which ended with the words, "Down with the war! Down with the government!"

In Russia the Bolsheviks had to operate illegally under Tsarism and faced being sent to the front, imprisoned in Siberia, or executed. In Italy repressive measures were taken against those attempting to leave a job and those advocating pacifism.

The myth of national unity

Considering the extent of propaganda and coercion, it is remarkable that so many resisted the war. At first the opposition was fragmented. In some places meetings were attacked and prominent individuals faced repression and imprisonment. This all went largely unreported thanks to censorship and press bias.

From the beginning anti-war activists were able to agitate in public, as shown in Ken Weller's book, *Don't be a Soldier!* The North London Herald League held its first anti-war street meeting in Haringey on the day war was declared and continued to hold regular meetings in Finsbury Park. It started out with around 50 members and although at first the meetings were sometimes attacked by "patriots", the anti-war activity in London grew rapidly in the first months of the war, as Ralph Fox describes:

> This anti-war activity in the early days of the war was not without its dangers...but although we got violent opposition we had enthusiastic support too. Our membership

mounted; from under 50 we reached a total of five or six hundred. From all over London, from the East End, from south and west came supporters who rallied to the anti-war standard, which was raised openly in Finsbury Park.[74]

In Glasgow John Maclean led the anti-war movement. On the day war was declared he was on holiday at Tarbert on the Firth of Clyde. He went around the town chalking the pavements with anti-war, anti-government slogans. He returned to Glasgow and immediately organised an open air meeting in Glasgow Green, where he argued a revolutionary, anti-war position.

Harry McShane, fellow BSP member and an engineering shop steward, recalls how, as the official left collapsed, Maclean pulled a movement together:

> John held Sunday afternoon meetings at Nelson's Monument throughout the war. He also started them in Bath Street, outside the army recruiting centre. Although the ILP (Independent Labour Party) wasn't doing much about the war, their best elements were coming to our meetings; so were the Socialist Labour Party members who were openly opposed to the war... John Maclean held the anti-war propaganda together.[75]

Maclean's factory gate meetings attracted hundreds of munitions workers at a time and were important in shaping the movement:

> Maclean demonstrated that the war was a war for trade and bought into full relief the sinister robber forces behind it. He gave example after example of the financiers and the big employers pointing a gun at the head of the government and demanding increased profits, and of other firms selling war materials to neutrals in the full knowledge that they were being resold to Germany. These examples were carried day after day into the factories.[76]

Empire and Revolution

Opposition to the war would grow more apparent and more powerful as the slaughter dragged on. The working class of Europe did not unanimously embrace the war with enthusiasm—even in the first months, before the terrifying scale of the slaughter and its terrible economic impact could really hit home.

6

Total war: keeping the home fires burning

"Almost everyone involved in the war thought it would be short. The German crown prince spoke of a 'bright, jolly war'. He expected a repetition of the Franco-Prussian War of 1870, when the French army was defeated within weeks. French soldiers wrote 'à Berlin' on the railway carriages taking them to the front. 'It will be all over by Christmas' was the common British refrain".[77]

The First World War involved the mass of the populations of all those countries which fought it. In France and Germany about 80 percent of males of military age were conscripted. Austro-Hungary mobilised 75 percent of its adult male population, while Britain, Serbia and Turkey called up between 50 and 60 percent. In Russia 16 million men served during the war.[78]

In India, far and away Britain's most important colony, sections of the privileged classes still clung to the British connection. When the war broke out even Mahatma Gandhi and B G Tilak, supporters of the campaign to boycott British goods, backed the British war effort. The Indian authorities mobilised enough recruits to massively expand the Indian army and many Indian troops were sent to join the carnage in Europe, while others fought in the Middle East.

The war was fought between two distinct blocs. On the Allied side were the three big imperialist powers of Britain, France and Russia, and from 1915 Italy, as well as Belgium,

Portugal, Greece, Romania, Serbia, Montenegro, Japan, Australia, Canada, New Zealand, India, Egypt, the West Indies and South Africa. In 1917, the United States declared war on Germany and joined the Allies.

These combined forces faced the Central Powers— Germany, the Austro-Hungarian Empire (a large area of central Europe ruled by the Hapsburg dynasty that included the modern Czech and Slovak Republics, Austria, Hungary, Slovenia, Croatia, Bosnia and parts of Romania and Poland), Turkey, with its Ottoman Empire, and Bulgaria.

It was the first modern industrial war between states of burgeoning economic strength and capacity. In 1887 Engels had predicted what this would mean: "Eight to ten million soldiers will slaughter each other and devour the whole of Europe until they have stripped it barer than any swarm of locusts has ever done". Twelve years later his view was supported by the detailed studies of a man who was neither a socialist nor a soldier—the Warsaw financier, Ivan Bloch. In an abridged version of his massive study, *Is War now impossible?* (1899), Bloch cited three reasons why a major European war would be unprecedented in scale and destructiveness.

Firstly military technology had transformed warfare to such an extent that a swift victory had to be ruled out. Secondly the massive increase in the size of the European armies and navies meant that any war would involve "as many as ten million men", with "the fighting spread over an enormous front" and "although there would be very high mortality rates...the next war would be a long war".

Thirdly, Bloch insisted, "economic factors would be the decisive and dominant element in the matter". War would mean "the entire dislocation of industry and severing of all sources of supply. The future of war is not fighting but famine, not the slaying of men but the bankruptcy of nations and the break-up of the whole social organisation".[79]

War on the home front

For Britain especially, previous wars had involved a professional army fighting in faraway lands and the conduct of these wars had little impact on the civil population. The industrialised warfare of the First World War was fundamentally different from everything that had gone before. If capitalist competition had caused the war, it also had to "keep the home fires burning". All economic life was subordinated to the war economy regardless of the impact on living standards.

Russia was regarded as relatively backward but, as Mike Haynes points out:

> Bertram D Wolfe was only slightly exaggerating when he said that *before* the revolution "the Russian state became the largest landowner, the largest trader, the largest owner of capital in Russia, or in the world. The needs of its huge armies made it the largest customer for private industry as well. This brought into being the world's largest apparatus of bureaucracy".[80]

Mass war needed mass production and industrial output was decisive. Early in the war German industrial superiority became evident when tens of thousands of British soldiers were killed at the front for lack of rifles, field guns and shells. The "shell scandal", as it became known, was a key factor in the fall of the Liberal government in May 1915 and its replacement by the National Government. Liberal Prime Minister Asquith was forced to form a national coalition with all the major parties, including the Labour Party. War production became the new cabinet's obsession.

Lloyd George was put in charge of the war drive and responded by reorganising the munitions industry.[81] The war in the trenches was accompanied by a domestic offensive against the working class to cut wages and increase the rate of exploitation. Industries producing consumer goods

Empire and Revolution

were turned over to munitions. Workers were shifted from industry to industry by state direction and fresh labour was found to replace those sent to the front. This meant mobilising not just soldiers to the front but workers into the war industries too.

It became clear to the generals and the politicians that success in the war required state control of the economy— regardless of free-market orthodoxy. The Ministry of Munitions was created in the face of resistance from some ultra conservative sections in the ruling class. But as Lloyd George made clear, "The Ministry was from the first to last a businessman organisation",[82] and this new capitalist high command, with its members drawn from the major arms industries, ran the show. The arms magnate Lord Weir of Cathcart, who owned one of the key munitions firms on Clydeside, would play a key government role in the attempts to smash shop floor organisation.

This wasn't a "national" government but a bosses' government, as Lloyd George proudly proclaimed: "No more remarkable collection of men was ever gathered together under the same roof. Between them they touched the industrial life of the country and of the Empire at every point. All the means of production, distribution and exchange were at their command".[83]

The servile state

The Defence of the Realm Act and the Munitions Act, along with the Treasury Agreement signed between the government and the union leaders in March 1915, gave the government the power to outlaw strikes, impose compulsory arbitration and forbid any worker to leave employment in a factory until granted a state permit to do so. These measures combined to remove fundamental rights from the working class at a time when the ruling class was introducing "dilution"—the introduction of unskilled men and women into work previously done by skilled engineers. Dilution on the bosses' terms was an immediate assault on the wages and conditions of the skilled workers. But there was no guarantee this was just for the duration of the war—it could weaken traditional bargaining power and jeopardise jobs in the future.

The strategy was to increase the level of industrial investment and simultaneously increase the rate of exploitation of the workforce. The pacifist Bertrand Russell defined the objective of such a war economy as; "maximum slaughter at minimum expense".[84]

Across Europe "social peace" was declared as the leaders of the working class collaborated with government and employers to keep order at home while workers were sent to the slaughter.

By 1917 a British war cabinet report acknowledged that state control "covered not only the national activities directly affecting the war effort, but every section of industry".[85] By the end of the war the government purchased 90 percent of all imports and marketed 80 percent of all food.

The war eventually consumed 70 percent of everything that was produced in Britain and this "war economy" was replicated all over Europe. In Germany Generals Hindenburg and Ludendorff exercised a virtual dictatorship over much of the economy in the later stages of the war.

In Britain strike leaders faced imprisonment under the Defence of the Realm Act, while in Germany "agitators" were conscripted to the front. Wages were controlled while rents, prices and profits were allowed to soar. Labour historian James Hinton coined the term "the servile state" and described its British manifestation as follows:

The collaboration of employers, state and trade union officialdom presaged the growth of a bureaucratic regulation

of every aspect of economic life and the withering away of
social and political freedoms... It was a war whose fate was
decided as much in the workshops of Britain and Germany
as it was in the trenches of France... The context of blood
and iron is at the same time the context of intensified social
discipline, of domestic repression.

A munitions worker, through most of the war, could
expect to escape the particular horror of the trenches but
there was no exemption from the generalised violence of
war. War brutalised and simplified social relations—at
home as well as on the front. It lent some of its own violence
and its own urgency to the workers' perennial fight for economic security and for class power.[86]

Women workers

The war transformed the lives of millions of women in
Britain and across the world. Women played a crucial role
on the home front. Up until 1914 the two major employers of
women were the textile industry and domestic service. The
female workforce grew massively during the war, especially
after conscription was introduced in 1916 and more men
were required at the front.

The figures are astonishing. Between 1914 and 1918 the
numbers of women in jobs rose by 1,345,000 and of these
over 95 percent were employed to fill the jobs of men who
were at war. In 1914 there were 385,000 women in unions
affiliated to the TUC; by 1918 this had risen to 1,086,000.
Some 750,000 women worked in munitions factories;
594,000 in engineering; 170,000 in machine shops.

Woolwich Arsenal became the biggest munitions factory in the world. In 1914 it employed 14,000 men and less
than 100 women. By 1918 it was bursting at the seams, with
more than 100,000 workers, half of them women. A third of
the workers in the new aircraft industry were women.[87] As
Lindsey German writes:

Increasingly, munitions relied on women with the proportion of women in national shell factories rising from 13 percent in 1914 to 73 percent in 1917. The Scottish munitions factory at Gretna employed 10,687 women in 1917, of that total 5,000-6,000 lived in hostels on site. Women war workers who worked in a munitions factory in London's Grays Inn Road made fuses for shells and apart from the toolmakers and foremen all the staff were female.[88]

War work was dirty and dangerous with women sometimes working a 14-hour day and often at lower rates of pay than the men. Accidents and explosions were common but were hushed up by government censors. But the war led to greater recognition that women could and should do "men's" jobs and that they should receive decent wages and equal pay for doing so.

Before the war 1.7 million women had been in domestic service and treated as skivvies—subject to very low pay, petty and constant supervision and with little free time. Vast numbers of them gladly left for the better pay and the greater personal freedom of factory work.

The state even provided limited services to make the long shifts possible for women. Some munitions factories had a workplace nursery and mothers who worked nightshifts got an extra childcare allowance.

In addition to the huge numbers drafted into munitions, women war workers included postwomen, the Land Army working in agriculture, delivery drivers, lorry drivers, bus and tram drivers and conductors and clerical workers. Thousands of women became nurses, with substantial numbers living on the battlefronts, directly experiencing the horrors of the war.

Specifically female services were established to fill support roles and free men for military combat—the Women's Royal Auxiliary Corps was attached to the army and then the Navy (WRNS) and the air force (WRAF). In both Britain and

Empire and Revolution

France the female workforce grew from 26 percent of the total workforce in 1914 to 37 percent in 1918. In Germany the numbers were even higher—the proportion of female workers rising from 35 percent to 55 percent over the same period.

America goes to war

The First World War was especially good for American capitalism. In 1914 the US was already the world's leading industrial power and although it remained neutral until 1917, the stimulus of war led to a boom in employment and investment. Between 1914 and 1916 Britain, France and Russia all depended heavily on US manufacturing, food and credit. In the absence of German competition, the US oil, chemicals, steel and shipbuilding industries flourished. US agriculture, after a long recession, enjoyed vast increases in demand and prices. Wheat rose from $0.70 per bushel in 1913 to $2.20 in 1917.

When the US declared war on Germany in April 1917 it too had to convert to a war economy and the federal government's attitude towards free enterprise went into reverse. It took over communications and railways, controlled the production of food and fuel, and regulated labour and all foreign trade. The war stimulated the changes already underway such as assembly line production. It also brought massive social change for women and the mass movement of southern black workers and agricultural labourers to northern cities. The war brought great prosperity to America but it was ill-divided; it went to the already wealthy bosses, not the poor. In 1916 Rockefeller became the world's first billionaire and by 1919 the US had 21,000 new millionaires.

An unofficial movement

In every state at war the demand for output of armaments in ever greater quantities meant a rapid speed up in working practices; the lifting of all restrictions on production;

the use of new machinery; and dilution. Working hours were extended with a 60-hour week common. The factories became more dangerous and exploitation more intense.

> War work was drawing women into munitions factories all across the world. Almost overnight a new sociology was taking shape in workplaces from Clydeside to the Danube: a core of skilled, male trade unionists alongside an unskilled mass of women and youths, with the women enjoying unprecedented levels of personal freedom. The official trade unions, full-square behind the war effort, refused to lift a finger to either defend the privileged status of the skilled men or protect the unskilled workers from exploitation. So an unofficial network of union shop stewards, known in German as Obluete or "confidential men", did the basic work of organising.[89]

To lead resistance the official trade union leaders would have had to call strikes that would have hindered the war effort. There was not a cat's chance in hell of that ever happening:

> The engineering union bureaucrats could choose whether or not to struggle but the engineers in the workshops could not. By withholding the strike weapon the officials had given the green light to an employers' offensive against all the customs and practises that engineers had painstakingly built up to make life a little more bearable under capitalism. Labour aristocrats they certainly had been, with better pay and conditions than many other workers. But now they were forced to fight and in so doing to take the lead in working class struggle. The officials had abandoned the membership. There was no alternative but to create an unofficial movement.[90]

In order to defend their position the craftsmen were forced to lead a much wider fight against the war economy and break from the old craft traditions. This meant drawing in the mass of the workforce, including the new, unskilled labourers.

It was an engineers' war and as producers of vital munitions they had real bargaining power. Workers who opposed the war built and led networks. They were often young and under the influence of revolutionary syndicalism—the idea of challenging capitalism through direct industrial action. They felt no allegiance to what they called "the labour lieutenants of capital" and were prepared to pressurise and if necessary defy the bureaucrats by organising the rank and file—even though most of those they worked alongside and represented felt they had to support "our boys at the front".

Shop stewards in the Glasgow munitions plants were forced to organise resistance six months into the war and from there came the first ever shop stewards' movement. In all the other key munitions centres—St Petersburg, Berlin, Budapest, Vienna, Turin, Sheffield, Barrow and Belfast—new bodies of workplace delegates were built from the local struggles against the war economy.

In Germany the revolutionary shop stewards built rank and file organisation that challenged the German state, while the metal workers in St Petersburg's enormously expanded engineering industry were the backbone of working class opposition to the Tsar. In Turin rank and file bodies known as internal commissions laid the basis for the workers' council movement that frightened the Italian bosses at the end of the war.

As 1915 wore on it became obvious that there would be no swift end to the war. Despite all the Allied efforts, the German front in France remained intact. Attacks on heavily defended German positions were proving hopeless and costly, without massive preliminary bombardment using hundreds of thousands of shells. The German generals faced the same problem. The demand for weaponry was escalating while the war was consuming soldiers much faster than voluntary recruitment could replace them. Necessity was driving the British government to conscription, while the need for greater output led to further regimentation in the factories.

Prices and profits

Prices had been rising in Britain from 1900; with the war they began to spiral. In the first 12 months of the war food prices rose by 32 percent while landlords jacked up rents. There were severe shortages and food rationing was introduced but there was no control over prices and rents. The same thing was happening all over Europe. Substitutes had to be found for foodstuffs and raw materials previously imported from enemy countries or subject to naval blockades.

As soldiers fell at the front and workers suffered at home, profits rose. From their own experiences ordinary people, especially women, began to see that the profiteers were benefiting from mass slaughter. The huge gap between the growing wealth of the rich and the suffering of the masses fuelled discontent. The lack of housing, overcrowding and unaffordable rents became unbearable. Grievances in the workplace and the wider community began to fuse.

Toni Sender was a young stenographer in a metal factory in Frankfurt where she set up an office workers' union. In 1910 she led a contingent of typists on their first demonstration:

It was then that we made our first acquaintance with the Prussian police truncheon...scores of armed police stopped us. "What have we done? Is the street forbidden to tax paying citizens?" I dared to ask. The answer was a rain of blows... With a small group of friends I talked with the librarian in the labour library and thus came into contact with books on socialism...we decided to meet in the park in the early morning before office hours to read and study together.[91]

Empire and Revolution

She joined the SPD and remembers the impact of the German party's vote for war: "The fourth of August brought a terrible blow. The German socialists had voted for the war credits! Everything seemed to collapse. How could they?".[92]

In the spring of 1915 Toni Sender slipped across the Swiss border to Zimmerwald to take part in the first international anti-war conference since hostilities erupted. She came back with the anti-war resolution in her toilet bag, which she then printed and distributed in large numbers on the streets of Frankfurt from beneath a long cape. She formed an anti-war group of women workers:

> We met every fortnight. I gave a short report of the news the authorities did not see fit to print. Most of the women were the wives of soldiers. Their loved ones were in the trenches. At home they endured near famine. Some of them were working in munitions factories. They had become emancipated and independent. Within a short period life had taught them what nobody had explained to them before.[93]

Within a year the war euphoria had evaporated. As the casualties and the economic hardships mounted the anti-war movement began to grow in all the main warring states. New struggles were about to erupt and out of them would grow new forms of organisation and resistance.

7

A long and murderous war of attrition

"Each side, as everybody knows, was counting on an early victory. One could quote innumerable evidences of such optimistic judgement. 'My French colleague', Buchanan [the British Ambassador in St Petersburg] writes in his memoirs, 'was at one moment so optimistic that he even bet me £5 that the war would be over by Christmas'.

"In his own heart Buchanan himself did not postpone the end of the war any later than Easter 1915. In opposition to this view we re-iterated day in and day out in our paper, from the autumn of 1914 on, that the war, regardless of all the official prophecies, would be hopelessly protracted and that all Europe would emerge from it utterly broken."
—*Leon Trotsky*[94]

The early predictions on both sides of a quick military victory proved utterly misplaced. In the first few months the German army raced through Belgium and northern France to within 50 miles of Paris, while on the Eastern Front the initial Russian advance against German lines drove west into East Prussia. But both advances were checked and forced back. After the battle of the Marne and the first battle of Ypres the Germans retreated to form a defensive line of trenches, while the Russians suffered terrible losses at the battles of Tannenberg and the Massurian Lakes and were driven back east out of German territory.

The pre-war military mind-set was the "cavalry charge",

but the war that was supposed to be over by Christmas became a war of attrition with the armies bogged down in unrelenting trench warfare that lasted another four years. It spread from the Eastern and Western fronts to the Italian-Austrian border, Greece and the Balkans, Turkey, Mesopotamia and Egypt.

In addition there was sporadic fighting in Togoland, South West Africa, East Africa, New Guinea and Samoa, China and the Pacific Islands. There was naval warfare too—in the Pacific, the Indian Ocean, the Falklands, the North Sea and the North Atlantic. The Allies imposed a naval blockade of Germany and Germany retaliated by launching a submarine war against Britain's merchant fleet. This drew the US into the war in 1917.

It is now estimated that the war killed 20 million people—at least 10 million military dead and the same number of civilians. The French lost almost 20 percent of their men of fighting age (1.4 million), the Russians 15 percent (2 million) and the Germans 13 percent (2 million). The British, too, lost almost an entire generation—750,000 men under the age of 30 killed and another 1.5 million permanently wounded (British figures include Ireland).

230,000 troops from the rest of the British Empire were killed. Of these India lost the greatest number, 75,000. Thousands of Indian soldiers were killed on the Western Front and there is a special Indian memorial at Neuve Chappelle.

Canada lost 65,000; Australia 62,000; New Zealand 18,000; and South Africa 9,500. West Indian troops numbering 15,600 volunteered and served on the Western Front as well as in Italy, Palestine and Mesopotamia.

The other military losses were: Austro-Hungary 1 million; Italy 460,000; Turkey 250,000; Bulgaria 80,000; the US 50,000; Serbia 45,000 and Japan 2,000. On average 5,600 soldiers were killed on each day of the carnage.[95] Scotland,

Turkey and Serbia had greater proportionate losses than any other nation. The Scots' mortality rate was one in four.

Life and death on the Western Front

In August 1914, right at the start of the war, the French lost over 140,000 men in five days as the German army drove deep into France. The German advance was halted at the Marne and the war of manoeuvre became a war of attrition as each side tried in vain to break through the entrenched position of the enemy. With their armies bogged down the generals devised ever more ambitious plans to achieve a breakthrough—all of them involved massive human sacrifice. Day after day, from both sides, thousands of men were hurled against enemy artillery and machine gun fire. The generals called it the "theory of the offensive"; in reality it meant callous, cavalier, suicide missions.

Millions of young men were undergoing experiences for which nothing in life had prepared them. Those who had been naïve enough in August 1914 to believe they were embarking on some great adventure realised they were simply cannon fodder and felt duped:

> It was mud, boredom, bad food and death all around them. For the working class or peasant conscripts of "the poor bloody infantry", it also involved the knowledge that life was very different from the generals and staff officers with good food and wine, comfortable billets and conscripted men to wait on them. This did not lead to automatic rebellion. Many of the conscripts came from backgrounds with no tradition of resistance to orders from above... Habits of deference could lead to men doggedly accepting their fate—especially when resistance would be met with military "justice".

> "The strange look on the faces of men waiting to go back to the front", noted the officer and war poet, Wilfred Owen,

"was not despair or terror, it was more terrible than terror, for it was a blindfold look and without expression, like a dead rabbit".[96]

Nonetheless the possibility of resistance and rebellion was always there as Christmas 1914 showed.

The generals were shocked when on Christmas Eve along parts of the German line soldiers put Christmas trees on the trench parapets. Troops on either side sang carols and applauded each other's efforts. On Christmas morning British and German soldiers climbed out of their trenches to fraternise, play football and bury their dead in no man's land.

This Christmas truce represented a serious threat to military discipline. Featured in Richard Attenborough's film version of *Oh! What a Lovely War* and in the more recent French film *Joyeux Noel* Christmas 1914 is one of the better known examples of fraternisation that became commonplace. In some areas the truce lasted well into January 1915 and in one section of the front it lasted into the middle of March. This was despite the efforts of both army commands to get the slaughter going again, with senior officers on both sides trying to force reluctant men to fight. British officers were ordered to shoot any soldiers fraternising with the enemy.

By 1915 patriotic zeal among the troops was rapidly diminishing on all sides. On the British side it was not difficult to see why.

Somehow it is hard to like First World War generals. In so many of their photographs they seem comfortable, secure and well breakfasted. Their uniform doesn't help. Breeched, booted and spurred, they ride or stride their way about a world of Châteaux and staff conferences. There is an age-old tension between the man on horseback and the man on foot; when mounted it is hard not to look, very literally, down on

A long and murderous war of attrition

those below. On the Western Front polished leather and tailored whipcord conveyed a message which muddy folk in khaki serge did not always welcome.[97]

On Christmas day while some frontline troops fraternised, British Commander Field Marshall Haig was dining on turtle soup, back at the Château.

In March 1915 German naval seaman Richard Stumpf wrote in his diary:

> A deep gulf has arisen between the officers and the men. The men are filled with undying hatred for the officers and the war. Everyone hopes for the return of peace. We don't even want to fight any more. We have had enough. Where's that wonderful enthusiasm of the August days?[98]

Disillusion also affected some of the middle class who held junior officer rank. Many came to hate and oppose the war and this is reflected in the work of the British war poets Siegfried Sassoon and Wilfred Owen, the German war poet Rainer Maria Rilke, and in the post-war writings of Ford Madox Ford (*Parade's End*, *The Good Soldier*), Robert Graves (*Goodbye to All That*), Erich Maria Remarque (*All Quiet on the Western Front*) and Henri Barbusse (*Under Fire*). In Lewis Grassic Gibbon's great socialist novel, *Sunset Song*, one of the most poignant moments is the execution of heroine Chris Guthrie's husband, Ewan, for desertion from the Western Front.

Slaughter at the Somme

The Battle of the Somme, launched on 1 July 1916, has come to epitomise the madness and horror of war. It was a huge offensive, pre-planned by the Allied High Command, aimed at destroying the enemy and achieving the kind of breakthrough that would hasten the end of the war.

In keeping with the mechanised nature of this new

warfare, the generals ordered railways built, cable laid and trenches dug on a mass scale, well in advance of the battle. Prior to the week-long bombardment of the German trenches, British sappers tunnelled underneath them to lay explosives. The British High Command convinced themselves that their massive bombardment would wipe out most of the enemy, destroy their machine gun posts, and allow the British foot soldiers to smash through defenceless German lines.

Those who went over the top on the first day of the Somme were led to believe by their commanders that they would meet with little or no German resistance. But they quickly discovered how badly they had been misled; the much vaunted artillery bombardment had been a failure—"impressive mainly for its noise".[99] Many of the shells were duds and failed to explode, while two-thirds were shrapnel—useless for destroying barbed wire or machine gun emplacements.

The Germans were well prepared and had fortified their defences with over 1,000 machine gun posts. 21,392 British soldiers were killed and another 35,493 wounded on that first day alone—a 50 percent casualty rate. The first day of the Somme saw the largest casualties in British military history. The losses in less than 15 hours add up to more than all the British casualties in the Crimean War, the Boer War and the Korean War put together.

The Germans, sheltering in fortified dug outs, emerged as the artillery barrage lifted to fire into the enemy lines. Their machine gunners watched in amazement as wave upon wave of British infantry was ordered across no-man's land, to be mowed down in the lethal German crossfire. A young infantryman later recalled, "The date 1 July is engraved in our hearts, along with the faces of our pals... We were two years in the making and ten minutes in the destroying".[100]

In the space of a few days three raw Australian divisions lost 23,000 young men at the Somme and with them their faith in British leadership: "If the Australians wish to trace their modern day suspicion and resentment of the British to a date and place," writes the Australian historian Peter Charlton, "then August 1916 and the village of Pozières are useful points of departure".[101]

The Somme was no picnic for the Germans either. Between July and September British gunners fired 6.5 million shells into their lines. The laying of mines underneath the German trenches was hazardous for the British sappers; for the German troops it created dread and carnage. A German officer described the battle landscape:

> The sunken road now appeared as nothing but a series of enormous shell holes filled with bits of uniform, weapons and bits of dead bodies. Among the living lay the dead. As we dug ourselves in we found them in layers stacked one on top of the other. One company after another had been shoved into the maelstrom and steadily annihilated.[102]

Fighting on the Somme raged from July to November 1916 and saw the "victors" gain six miles, but the British front line was still three miles short of Bapaume, the objective set for it on day one. Allied casualties for the battle totalled 600,000, two thirds of them British. The German figure was 650,000. A German officer described the Somme as, "The muddy grave of the German field army, and of confidence in the infallibility of German leadership".[103]

At the end of 1916, having presided over one military disaster after another, Herbert Asquith resigned as Prime Minister. He was replaced by Lloyd George. At the same time Lord Kitchener was sidelined. The cabinet had lost faith in him, and so had the soldiers at the front.

Verdun

In the big set-piece battles soldiers found themselves living below ground in rat and lice infested trenches, fighting knee

Empire and Revolution

deep in mud and facing terrifying new weaponry like rapid fire machine guns, tanks, flame throwers, poison gas, aerial bombing, exploding mines and constant shelling. Often soldiers had to fight wearing gas masks. It is estimated that 190,000 British soldiers were gassed. Of those who survived and seemed to recover, many would die young as the result of damaged lungs. The Allies used poison gas just as much as the Germans.

The battle of Verdun was especially brutal. The Germans launched a huge offensive in February 1916 and the fighting continued until December. Two million French and German soldiers fought what was the longest battle of the war. By its end half of them were dead and the battle lines were back to where they had been on the first day.

The battlefront at Verdun was so narrow and the concentration of men and shells so great that the combatants who survived recalled the terrible fear and claustrophobia caused by constant bombardment. For many survivors it meant shell shock.

> Men might be killed instantly, but without apparent damage, by concussion; blown to tatters by direct hits; cut up as if by some malicious butcher; crippled by flying fragments of their comrades' bodies or shocked into babbling incoherence by a capricious hit which left them unscathed among the remnants of their friends. Evidence of death was all too abundant; splintered trees turned to gibbets, heavy with dismembered limbs and glistening ropes of entrails. One French officer wrote of "a place where one can't possibly distinguish if the mud were flesh or the flesh were mud".[104]

Over 23 million shells were fired during the battle. Nine villages which had stood for a thousand years were destroyed and never rebuilt. The woods and fields were so badly polluted by metal, high explosives and bodies that they were beyond cultivation. Some of the soldiers who died there were buried in vast military cemeteries but the bodies of hundreds of thousands could not be identified. After the war an ossuary was built; it contains the bones of 130,000 unknown soldiers, French and German.

The Aisne Offensive and the French mutiny

The German and French casualties at Verdun were unprecedented, yet neither side made any gains. By the end of the battle the French had made extraordinary sacrifices to withstand then force back an enormous German assault, but it was an army running out of patience with its leaders. After the scale of French losses at Verdun there were serious doubts at the very top about the wisdom of launching a major spring offensive in 1917 against the German lines at the river Aisne.

The French government had fallen to be replaced by a new administration and political support for Army Chief General Nivelle's spring offensive was on the wane. The new French Minister of War soon discovered that even the army group commanders were unenthusiastic.

Nivelle intended to strike a sudden blow at the Germans who had retreated in good order to new defensive positions on the Hindenburg line. The offensive was to involve 27 French divisions. But the retreating Germans had left a desert behind them—roads, railways and bridges had been destroyed, orchards cut down, wells poisoned and booby traps left everywhere. When challenged by his War Minister, Nivelle insisted his grand plan would work. He argued a major breakthrough against the Germans would save Russia and win the war. Simply taking the territory the Germans had vacated would, for him, be "only a poor little victory. It is not for so meagre a result I have assembled here on the Aisne 1,200,000 soldiers, 5,000 artillery guns and 500,000 horses. The game would not be worth the candle".[105]

Empire and Revolution

Nivelle threatened to resign if his planned offensive did not go ahead and despite serious misgivings the French politicians and the British High Command agreed to it. The plan relied on surprise but it was a commodity in short supply. Two weeks before the attack the enemy had been fully briefed:

On 4 April the Germans had captured a copy of Nivelle's plan, which had unwisely been taken into a forward position. Soon they knew everything; date, times and objectives. This information was circulated to their gunners to enable them to shell the French trenches at their most vulnerable moment, just before the attack started... The prospects would have been poor even if security had remained intact... By now the course of tragedy was irrevocably set.

The attack went ahead on 16 April with the French infantry going forward into icy sleet:

The plan's sternest critics soon saw their fears confirmed. Even where they penetrated the defences they were taken on by flanking machine guns...or briskly counter-attacked by Germans who had sat out the bombardment in the huge limestone caverns above the Aisne. By nightfall, far from being deep in the German rear, the attack had stalled. The medical services, counting on light casualties envisaged by the plan, were overwhelmed... Nivelle refused to recognise the failure. He ordered more attacks in the face of evident catastrophe and then tried to blame his subordinate... Now his army, like a beast of burden flogged beyond endurance, began to mutiny.[106]

On 29 April an infantry battalion refused to go back up the line. Its ringleaders were arrested, four were shot and the remainder imprisoned. For a few days the episode was isolated but the mutiny soon spread. By the time the battle ended on 9 May, it had cost another 250,000 French lives.

An estimated 68 divisions, half the French army, refused to return to the front after the hated offensive. "Desertions from the front went up from an average of 1,437 to 2,625 in 1917 and from the rear they increased from an average of 15,745 to 27,579. Many wanted to march on Paris, chanted 'Down with the war' and sang the Internationale".[107]

The French mutiny lasted for over two months. In some units soviets were discussed and two regiments met and composed the following demands:

> We want peace... We've had enough of the war and we want the politicians to know it. When we go into the trenches we will plant a white flag on the parapet. The Germans will do the same and we will not fight until the peace is signed.

One soldier wrote, "I am ready to go into the trenches but we are doing like the clothing workers—we are going out on strike". He was inspired by news that women clothing workers in Paris had struck against the privations of war. In June two Russian brigades were moved to the military camp at La Courtine, 200 miles south of Paris and quickly established a soviet involving French soldiers:

> 10,000 men at La Courtine were heading for open revolt. "Down with the war!" said a notice over the door of the delegates' hut. Passing round the units was a proclamation from Russia, "Declaration of Soldiers' Rights", which advocated free speech and revolution.[108]

As a sop to the mutineers Nivelle was removed and replaced as Commander in Chief by General Pétain, who had commanded the defence of Verdun. A combination of concessions and repression restored order: 3,500 soldiers were court martialled, 550 condemned to death and 49 actual death sentences carried out. This was limited punishment given the scale of the mutiny. Clearly it had terrified the French generals and the ruling class.

The British offensive and the mutiny at Étaples

In May 1917 the wily Pétain opted for caution and planned to sit tight and wait for the imminent arrival of US troops. Haig, Pétain's less shrewd counterpart, was not prepared to forgo the offensive and see the Americans "steal the glory". So he launched a British led campaign in Flanders that led to a series of bloody battles at Arras, Vimy, Passchendaele and Cambrai.

Mutiny was not confined to the French army that year. Thanks to Haig, British, Australian and New Zealand troops mutinied in September, launching a bloody five-day revolt involving 100,000 troops at the hated base camp at Étaples, near Boulogne. The mutineers locked the officers in the guard room and set fire to the accommodation huts of the hated British Military Police. Some of the rebels joined other Allied mutineers in Paris and there was talk of setting up soviets, inspired by events in Russia.

But like their French counterparts the British generals ended the rebellion by making concessions and executing the leaders. Unlike the French they succeeded in keeping a lid on the whole affair until long after the war.[109] The story was retold in the wonderful BBC TV drama, *The Monocled Mutineer*, broadcast in 1986.

Passchendaele was the third of four separate battles fought at Ypres in western Belgium. A big battle was fought there in each of the years 1914, 1915, 1917 and 1918. The 1917 battle lasted from July to November and became notorious because of the particularly appalling conditions. By 1917 the British field gunners were firing 500,000 shells a day and million-shell days were quite common. During the battle of Passchendaele there were days when two million shells were fired.

1917 saw the wettest autumn in memory and the prolonged, torrential rain turned the battlefield into a quagmire. The battle culminated in the terrible struggle to capture the village of Passchendaele where men, equipment and horses were drowned in the mud and where the dead became stepping stones for the living.

Stalemate, disillusion and mass desertion

Allied hopes of victory on the Western Front in 1917 had perished with the failure of Nivelle's spring offensive and the mass mutinies affecting nearly half the French regiments. Although the British mutiny was kept secret, Haig's Flanders campaign of 1917 proved futile and costly and contributed to the growing disenchantment with the war in both Britain and France. The feeling was even greater in Russia, where it helped topple the Romanov dynasty in February and would lead to the overthrow of the Kerensky government in October. The summer of 1917 severely shook the confidence of the ruling classes, with mutinies, strikes and the Russian Revolution making a big impact at home and on every battle front.

The longer the stalemate dragged on the more the soldiers' resentment grew and the greater their reluctance to continue fighting. This was particularly true on the German side. That same summer the Saxon and Württemberg units of the German army mutinied too. But it was through mass desertions and mass "stay-aways" by army conscripts and reservists that German opposition to continuing the war expressed itself. Nick Howard describes the scale of desertion:

Mass desertion by Germans in the west is overlooked by historians. Yet in 1917-1918 more than two million soldiers deserted in what one German researcher in the 1920s, called "the hidden military strike". The huge task of transportation that characterised German mass mobilisation facilitated desertion. Journeys between, to and from the fronts were by train and reports from the General Staff in the autumn of 1917 complained of unrest and mutiny on the trains, leading to a loss of 10 percent of replacement soldiers during train journeys. In May 1918 the Swiss government tightened its controls over the 25,000 German deserters it gave sanctuary, as the Bolsheviks were instigating many of them to become "world revolutionaries".

Desertion grew into mass revolt and brought the war to a halt a full year before the plans of the Allied Powers could mature for a victorious offensive with American support in the summer of 1919. From 1917 onwards desertion by stay-at-homes and shirkers drastically reduced the offensive capacity of the German armies in the west.

They were, by their actions, equally as instrumental in fomenting major political changes as were their Russian counterparts. German deserters as mutineers at one end of the scale of activity and as draft dodgers at the other, through their soldiers' councils challenged the political structures of the social democratic government that was given power on 9 November 1918.[110]

Despite the evidence of extensive German desertion, historians choose to point triumphantly to a hard fought victory by the Allies with very high casualty rates up to the moment of the Armistice. The attempt to show that there was no movement by German soldiers to desert in the last year of the war is quite simply a cover-up. German nationalists glorified the "front soldier" and falsified the army's record in the field by creating the myth of "the stab in the back", which alleged that liberals, pacifists, Jews and socialists in the homeland alone had brought defeat on the German army. This was part of Hitler's rant against the communists and the Jews.

British historians who dismissed this myth, nevertheless gave it weight when they argued that of all the armies in the field, the German army was the one that never cracked. Nevertheless it was a myth and an insult to the ordinary German soldiers who opposed the continuation of the slaughter.

Historians record the fears of the German General Staff over declining morale in the German armies and their frequent complaints of "Drückeberger" or shirking, but ignore the desertion and absenteeism that were the most pervasive symptoms of this malaise in the last years of the war. Historians have concentrated on the mutiny in the fleet at Kiel as the main factor in the collapse of the Kaiser regime, allocating a conservative role to the rank and file in the army who nevertheless built 10,000 revolutionary soldiers' councils.[111]

8

A global war

Although, from British, French and German viewpoints, the Western Front—a 500 mile line of trenches stretching from the North Sea coast of Belgium to Switzerland—was the principle theatre of the war, it was not the only one. The war encompassed much of the world.

It was fought bitterly on the Eastern Front in East Prussia, Poland and Russia as well as in Italy, Austro-Hungary, Greece, Romania, Macedonia, Serbia, Albania, Bulgaria, Turkey, Palestine, Egypt, Syria, Mesopotamia (now Iraq), Persia (now Iran), Africa, China and in the Pacific Islands.

On the Eastern Front Germany and Austro-Hungary fought Russia and a higher proportion of those who fought were killed than on the Western Front. Two million Russian soldiers died. As the Russian army was driven back eastwards across Poland during the summer of 1915, thousands of refugees, their homes and villages destroyed, headed for the cities.

The military catastrophe at the front exposed the incompetence of Russia's autocratic regime but Tsar Nicholas II had neither the will nor the wit to change. Instead of liberalising the regime he decided to rule like a true despot, taking personal command of the imperial army. In his absence the Tsarina and her faith-healer Rasputin began to exercise a disastrous influence over the domestic government and the Russian bourgeoisie was in despair. In the early spring of 1916 the French generals pleaded with their Russian allies to mount an attack that would divert German troops from the murderous battle at Verdun on the Western Front. The

Russians agreed and planned to advance and recapture the key railhead at Vilna (Vilnius).

They launched their offensive in March but the German commanders had two weeks' advance warning of the plan of attack due to the lack of internal security. The Russian attacks were mown down and their troops shelled by German artillery. In this battle Russia lost 110,000 men, including 12,000 deaths from frostbite. A Russian army of 300,000 had been routed by 50,000 Germans and the debacle left the Russian troops in the sector badly demoralised.

For a while Russia fared better further south in Galicia against the Austrians. They almost destroyed the Austrian army and German forces had to be rushed in to stabilise the situation as Czechs and Ruthenes deserted en masse from the Austro-Hungarian armies. The Russian advance encouraged Romania to join the war on the Allied side but the Austro-German counter offensive saw the Russian and Romanian forces badly beaten. Most of Romania was over-run and Russia had almost reached the end of its tether. On the home front the lack of food and fuel, the collapse of the transport system and rampant inflation contributed to the February Revolution.

In March the Tsar abdicated and the provisional government took power. It continued with the war and launched another futile offensive in July but a German victory virtually ended Russia's military campaign as tens of thousands of Russian troops deserted the front. By voting with their feet, they helped topple the Tsar and halted Prime Minister Kerensky's efforts to prolong the war. Though peasant soldiers were predominant among Russian deserters, their actions advanced the workers' revolution.

Italy sides with the highest bidder

Before 1914 Italy had entered into an alliance with Germany and Austria, hoping to gain territories in the Balkans and along its Alpine border. But when war broke out it refused to honour that alliance and touted itself round the European capitals seeking the best rewards for joining the bloodbath. Italy was divided. The Italian parliament and the Italian Socialist Party were against the war. But the right wing, the King and sections of big business, encouraged by British and French financial subsidies, were demanding the government declare war on the side of France and Britain.

In May 1915, as parliament hesitated, the Italian right took to the streets. Aided and abetted by the police and the army and bankrolled by big business, the pressure they exerted was enough to swing the vote in favour of war.

In the working class citadel of Turin there was a general strike against war but the city's working class was eventually isolated and left to resist alone.

The First World War had a profound economic and social impact in Turin. This was partly because Italy joined the alliance against Germany only in 1915, which had allowed time for the true horror of the war to become apparent.

A few days before Italy's declaration of hostilities against Austria and Germany a spontaneous general strike swept the city as workers fought on the streets against pro-war campaigners. While many ranks of the Second International had been crushed by the steamroller of imperialism, Turin's socialists threw themselves onto the barricades and battled to resist the violent repression that followed.[112]

Italy joined the Allies in the hope of gaining territory at Austria's expense. The Italian industrialists made vast profits from the war; some, like tyre manufacture Pirelli, by selling tyres and raw materials to their German enemy via neutral Switzerland.

Although Italy ended up on the winning side, the war was a disaster for most Italians. Industrial workers were badly needed in the munitions plants, so peasant conscripts were herded into a series of futile assaults on Austro-German positions in the frozen Alpine passes, under the leadership of the privileged and corrupt officer class. In October 1917 an Austro-German attack broke through at Caporetto and 300,000 Italian troops surrendered and a similar number deserted. The routed Italian army fell back almost to Venice and Italy faced defeat. The Central Powers had already defeated Serbia (in 1915), Romania (in 1916) and Russia (in 1917). In the aftermath of Caporetto the Italian government launched a rapid industrial expansion and placed the northern factories under military discipline, with working hours increased and strikes outlawed.

Early in 1917, 50,000 Italian troops mutinied; wage strikes broke out in the northern cities in response to 80 percent food price inflation; and there were protests and riots over bread shortages led by working class women. May Day 1917 saw the start of anti-war demonstrations that grew in size, reaching their peak in the summer in Turin. Again working class women and young people played a vital part in them.

The demand for minority national rights inspired the sudden mass desertion of Czech soldiers from the Austrian armies. This and other mass desertions on the East European front accelerated the collapse of the Hapsburg Empire. By November 1918, with the help of French, British and colonial troops from the Caribbean, the Italians were able to finally grind down the weakened Austro-Hungarian army and force its surrender. German generals described their military alliance with Austro-Hungary as "like being tied to a corpse".

Italy would end the war with more artillery than Britain and as an exporter of military trucks to its allies. But Italian bosses would face an angry, militant working class, while the landowners would face embittered, landless peasant soldiers returning from the war.

Empire and Revolution

Gallipoli

Turkey entered the war in October 1914. An attempted Turkish invasion of Russia was checked and in January 1915 the Russians counter-attacked, shattering the Turkish 3rd Army, which suffered 90,000 casualties. When Turkey then received German assistance the Russians asked for Allied help.

In February 1915 the Allies launched a naval assault and an amphibious landing on the Gallipoli peninsula in the narrow straits of the Dardanelles. Encouraged by naval minister Winston Churchill the assault was aimed at capturing Constantinople and taking Turkey out of the war. Historian Hew Strachan explains:

> Lord Kitchener, the Secretary of State for War, was not optimistic, not least because the small British army, depleted by fierce fighting at Ypres on the Western Front in November 1914, was fully committed in France. But he recognised that if such an operation were to be mounted its best choice of target would be the Dardanelles "particularly if...reports could be spread at the same time that Constantinople was threatened". Kitchener had opened a door wide enough for his counterpart at the Admiralty to force entry.
>
> Winston Churchill had been chafing at the bit since the war's beginning. Wireless telegraphy had enabled him to intervene in operational matters, not always with the happiest of results... But it had not abated his thirst for battle. To his chagrin, more action had come the army's way than the navy's and he felt particularly keenly the humiliation the senior service had already suffered at the hands of the Turks. Here was an opportunity to right the situation.
>
> In its pre-war planning the navy had considered the possibility of amphibious assaults against Germany on the Baltic coast; to apply these principles to Turkey and the Dardanelles seemed logical not only to him but also to

Jackie Fisher, restored in August 1914 as First Sea Lord. In operational terms the project was guided by a great deal of wishful thinking.[113]

Churchill's concern was more the safeguarding of British interests in Egypt and the wider Middle East than in helping Russia, but the operation was a disaster. Gallipoli cost over 157,000 lives before it was finally abandoned, with the surviving Allied troops eventually evacuated in December 1915, many of them wounded and suffering from dysentery. The Turkish troops saw off the assault, but their casualties were greater—87,000 compared to the Allies' 70,000.

Although the Australian and New Zealand losses were fewer in number than their British and French allies, they were catastrophic in proportion to their tiny populations. The Gallipoli fiasco contributed to the downfall of Asquith's Liberal government and Churchill's failure to gain a cabinet post in the National Government that replaced it in December 1915.

War in the Middle East and the Balkans

One lesson that the British did learn from Gallipoli was that instead of overstretching British forces, it would try to coerce India, by a combination of reform and repression, to provide a huge number of troops to protect British interests in the Middle East against the threat posed by Turkey and the Ottoman Empire. This "carrot and stick" approach was the bedrock of British Indian Policy during the rest of the war.

The crucial watershed in the British conduct of the war came with Asquith's replacement by Lloyd George in December 1916. The new Prime Minister regarded the Dominions with the hard, covetous gaze of the recruiting-sergeant. The Empire in short was to underwrite the extended belligerency on which the Lloyd George coalition was based.

Empire and Revolution

Before 1916, Britain was at war, assisted by her Empire; subsequently the Empire was at war, orchestrated by Britain.[114]

By 1918 India had one million troops serving in the major theatres of the First World War, with 80 percent of them in Egypt, Palestine, Mesopotamia and the Persian Gulf; 15 percent in France and the remainder in East Africa. "The true worth of the Indian army to Britain lay in its reserve role that allowed British troops to be diverted to France from East Africa, Palestine and Egypt".[115]

In 1916 Turkey had launched an attack on the Suez Canal, but increasingly reliant on the use of Indian troops and aided by an Arab uprising against the Ottoman Empire, forces under British command were eventually able, after a series of early setbacks, to defeat the Turkish armies in Egypt, Palestine and Mesopotamia by 1918. Official estimates record that 250,000 Turkish troops were killed in the war and that two million civilians died as a result of it. But as Hew Strachan argues, "Total Turkish deaths in the war may have risen as high as 2.5 million, more than three times those of Britain and in some villages only 10-20 percent of those of military age returned from war".[116] In Turkey the price of bread rose fifty-fold between 1914 and 1918. "An inadequate internal transport system had left Constantinople dependent on imported food even in peacetime. During the war the blockade increased the city's reliance on its hinterland but Anatolia had been sucked dry of its principle resource—men".[117]

The war had originated in the Balkans and fighting began there early. The Austrian invasion of Serbia led to the capture of Belgrade but the Austrian advance stalled in the face of fierce Serbian resistance and the Serbs recaptured the city. However, the Allied failure at Gallipoli encouraged Bulgaria, with its territorial ambitions in the Balkans, to join the Central Powers. A combined German, Austrian and

Bulgarian attack crushed the Serbian resistance and Serbia surrendered in 1915.

Fighting broke out between Greece and Bulgaria over the Greek province of Macedonia. Allied forces helped Greece to force Bulgaria to surrender in autumn 1917.

The war in Asia

Japan, a growing military power, had already surprised the world by winning the Russo-Japanese war in 1905. Japan's foreign minister in 1914 had previously served as an ambassador in London and was an ardent Anglophile. He believed Japan could be a great imperialist power like Britain.

On 23 August Japan declared war on Germany. It had every intention of keeping its involvement limited, though later in 1917 it deployed a squadron of ships in the Mediterranean. The biggest of the German overseas naval bases was at Tsingtao in China. In 1914 Japan immediately set about the capture of Tsingtao from its German garrison by an amphibious assault that breached China's neutrality. The fact that the British contributed two battalions to a Japanese force of 60,000 meant Britain had colluded, not for the last time in this war, in infringing the rights of neutrals—the very principle the British cabinet had ostensibly gone to war to defend.

In November the Germans surrendered at Tsingtao and the Japanese were the only troops who were actually home by Christmas. Japanese total losses in the First World War were 2,000. By 1916 the elder statesmen and elements in the army had re-asserted their hold on government. Admirers of Germany rather than Britain, they began to focus on what they saw as a coming struggle with the United States.

The Japanese Navy also used the opportunity to seize the German Pacific Islands north of the equator. Britain could hardly protest when "its own dominions similarly seized the opportunity to further their colonial ambitions. New Zealand

Empire and Revolution

had occupied Samoa by 30 August, 1914 and Australia had laid claim to New Guinea and the Solomon Islands".[118]

But British anxieties were focused on the activities of the Japanese army in Asia. China was already in chaos following the revolution of 1911 and the fall of the Manchu dynasty. Its internal divisions created Japan's opportunity to advance its indirect control over the remainder of China. The Japanese economy boomed in the First World War, not least on the back of Japanese investment in China and the exploitation of its labour and raw materials.

In August 1917 China abandoned its neutrality. "Its declared enemy was Germany but the real danger came from Japan. Its purpose was not to fight in the war but to attend the peace conference in order to regain Shantung and re-assert its sovereignty".[119]

Non-combatant labour: exploitation and racism
Aside from the Allied troops who were doing the fighting, the British High Command brought in thousands of workers to service the battlefronts—especially in France and Belgium.

Accommodation and fortifications had to be built; thousands of miles of trenches had to be dug; roads, railways and canals had to be built and maintained; telephone lines and cabling had to be installed; and ships, trains and trucks had to be loaded and unloaded at the docks, railheads and distribution centres. Military equipment had to be maintained and horses had to be fed and looked after. In addition to these essential tasks, the generals and senior officers were cosseted behind the frontlines with 65,000 men and women servants allocated to wait on them.

All of this ancillary work required huge amounts of labour and increasingly the generals could not afford to use their combat forces on such work. Initially it was undertaken by labourers and tradesmen sent from Britain and grouped into Labour Companies of the Army Service Corps. Latterly it included women workers, organised in the Women's Auxiliary Corps.

The same kind of process took place in all the other belligerent nations. As the war dragged on the demand for non-combatant labour grew and the British commanders decided its numbers should be supplemented by men who were medically graded as unsuitable for combat, by captured enemy prisoners, and by conscientious objectors from home.

Despite all of these measures the chronic shortage of labour persisted and workers from all parts of the British Empire, notably China, Egypt and the West Indies, were brought mainly to France to work on the Western Front. It is estimated that as many as 100,000 labourers came from the colonies and there is plenty of evidence to show they were treated badly and subjected to racism.

In 1917 Chinese and Egyptian dockworkers drafted in to the port of Boulogne by the British came out on strike alongside British and Commonwealth Army mutineers at Étaples. Field Marshall Haig ordered reprisals in which 27 of these strikers were shot dead.[120]

West Indian volunteers resist racism

Thousands of West Indians volunteered to join the British army and were encouraged to do so by Marcus Garvey, on the basis that they would win the right to be treated as equals.[121] Lord Kitchener, the face on the "your country needs you" poster, refused to countenance black troops at the front but King George's intervention—combined with the desperate need for men—made it happen despite the ingrained racism of the War Minister.

So in 1915 the British West Indies Regiment (BWIR) was formed by grouping together the Caribbean volunteers. Their initial journey to England was perilous, with hundreds of soldiers suffering from severe frostbite when their ships

Empire and Revolution

were diverted via Halifax, Nova Scotia. Arriving in the war zone, they found that the fighting was to be done by white soldiers, while they were assigned the dirty and dangerous work of loading ammunition, laying telephone wires and digging trenches.

Throughout the war, 15,600 men in the regiment's 12 battalions served with the Allied forces, two thirds of the volunteers coming from Jamaica and the rest from Trinidad and Tobago, Barbados, the Bahamas, British Honduras (now Belize), Grenada, British Guiana (now Guyana), the Leeward Islands, St Lucia and St Vincent.

As well as serving in France, the BWIR played a vital role in active combat against the Turkish army in Palestine, Jordan, Mesopotamia and Egypt. They also served in northern Italy.

In November 1918, the nine BWIR battalions that had served in France and Italy were concentrated at the port of Taranto in southern Italy to prepare for demobilisation. They were joined by the three BWIR battalions that had served in Egypt and Mesopotamia. Severe labour shortages at Taranto meant the West Indian troops were made to carry out the arduous work of loading and unloading ships, as well as the demeaning task of building and cleaning toilets for white soldiers, who were given a pay rise while the black soldiers were not.

For the BWIR troops this was the final indignity. They mutinied against racist discrimination and refused to work. After four days a battalion of the Worcestershire Regiment was despatched to restore order and the "ringleaders" were rounded up. 60 West Indian soldiers were later tried for mutiny and those convicted received sentences ranging from three to five years. One man got 20 years and another was executed by firing squad. In 1918 thousands of demobilised West Indian troops took their revenge in the widespread strikes and anti-colonial rioting that rocked the West Indies.

By the end of the war the motley Labour Corps that had initially begun with labourers and tradesmen sent from Britain, had grown to huge proportions, eventually numbering 390,000. At critical moments men from the Labour Corps were armed and fought as infantry. Over 5,000 of them died in the war and of those 2,500 were recorded as killed in action or dying from wounds.[122]

Civilian casualties

In addition to the massive death toll of those who fought in all the theatres of war can be added the 62,000 US soldiers who died of flu; the 2 million Russian civilians killed; the 82,000 civilians killed in Serbia (compared to the 45,000 soldiers); the 1.5 million Armenians killed between 1914 and 1918 in a genocide caused by the bloody fight to forge a nation out of the Ottoman empire;[123] and the 750,000 German civilians who died as a result of the Allied naval blockade.[124]

This blockade succeeded in restricting vital supplies and starved large numbers of the German population. It continued long after the signing of the armistice in November 1918 and had already contributed greatly to the reduction of food supplies to the Central Powers by over 50 percent in the final year of the war.

Long after the war ended famine encroached upon the civilian populations of Central Europe. The excuse given by the Allied victors for prolonging their barbaric blockade of Germany was that it would prevent the resurgence of German military power and suppress the revolutionary upheavals in Germany and in the states of the former Austro-Hungarian Empire.

The First World War created 5 million refugees. It dislocated society and spread famine, disease and poverty. After four years of horror and misery, which forced mass movements of people between and across continents, the world

Empire and Revolution

was ripe for a pandemic. It took the form of a virulent strain of influenza known as the Spanish Flu.

The first wave began either in the US or in the US army camps in northern France in 1918, killing 62,000 US soldiers—more than were killed in battle. It rapidly spread and another wave in the spring of 1919 ravaged the malnourished civilian populations of Europe. It then spread across the globe, killing an estimated 21 million people.

The First World War was the greatest tragedy the peoples of Europe had suffered since the Black Death in the 14th century.

9

Britain: the first sparks of resistance

"Like revolution, war forces life, from top to bottom, away from the beaten track. But revolution directs its blows against the established power. War, on the contrary, at first strengthens the state power which, in the chaos engendered by war, appears to be the only firm support—and then undermines it".[125]

—*Leon Trotsky*

Class consciousness reasserts itself

The expansion of mass production during the war undermined the position of the skilled craftsmen, creating new layers of unskilled and semi-skilled workers drawn from among women and from the countryside. The massive influx of new labour into the cities made the overcrowded slum housing even worse. Private landlords forced up rents and threatened to evict the most vulnerable.

By early 1915 ordinary people began to realise it was going to be a long, bloody war. There was desperation but there was also anger at the growing disparity between the sacrifices working people were expected to make and the enormous profiteering of big business and the rich.

Within a year class consciousness began to reassert itself. At first the resistance was directed at the immediate economic effects of war, but as the slaughter continued the resistance increasingly challenged the war itself. Between 1915 and 1917 numbers of strikes in Britain, Russia, Germany,

France and Italy increased dramatically—especially among the male workers under least pressure to join the army, the skilled metal workers essential to the war effort.

The unofficial networks of rank and file activists in engineering—shop stewards in cities like Glasgow, Sheffield, Berlin and Vienna—developed and remained intact, despite state repression and the hostility of their own trade union leaders. "The shop stewards' movement was a child of war. Its power was the power of munitions workers in a war whose fate was decided as much in the workshops of Britain and Germany as in the trenches of France".[126]

The strikes were accompanied by spontaneous protests led by working class women in the communities that were bearing the brunt of the war—the great Glasgow rent strike of 1915; the peace demonstrations in Germany from 1915 onwards; the protests over food shortages in many German towns and cities in the winter of 1916-17; and the bread riots and anti-war protests in Turin and St Petersburg in 1917.

In Britain the introduction of conscription in March 1916 led to further strikes and there was a rapid increase in the numbers of men prepared to defy or dodge the call-up. The growing resistance on the home front was accompanied by disillusion and war-weariness on all the battlefronts. The changing mood expressed itself in different ways: insubordination, desertion and, by early 1917, open mutiny. In taking the road of revolt individual soldiers and sailors were risking their lives.

Glasgow: the birth of Red Clydeside

The shop stewards' movement originated on the Clyde and it was born out of the first industrial revolt of the war. A key munitions centre, Glasgow had a high proportion of skilled workers and a large proportion of its workforce organised in very large workplaces. Glasgow also had a tradition of shop floor organisation; by 1914 Beardmore's Parkhead Forge and J G Weir's of Cathcart—two of the key factories—had functioning shop stewards' committees, which was unusual at the time.

The Clydeside engineers with their relative job security and high wages were seen as conservative and elitist in outlook. But wartime conditions and the attempt to destroy previously established working practices pushed them into resistance against the impact of the war economy and eventually against the war itself.

Crucially important was the presence of individual socialists, rooted in the key munitions plants. Most saw themselves as revolutionaries and were members of the British Socialist Party (BSP) or the Socialist Labour Party (SLP), while a few belonged to the bigger Independent Labour Party (ILP). The majority were shaped by the new syndicalism and by the regular Marxist economic classes run by the anti-war socialist John Maclean. When they united they punched way above their weight, with an influence on events that was disproportionate to their numbers.

The Glasgow engineers' pay claim provided the spark for the first strike of the war in February 1915. Sharp price rises and shortages affected skilled workers as well as the poor. In engineering there had been a national pay agreement which had expired and in Glasgow the local branches of the Amalgamated Society of Engineers, the main engineering union, were demanding an increase on the hourly rate. But the government and the employers, who were making huge profits, were determined to drive down wages, attack conditions and destroy shop floor organisation.

The employers rejected the wage claim for an extra two pence an hour while top union officials opposed their members' claim and agreed a no-strike deal with the government; even the local union officials refused to do anything. Meanwhile Maclean and individuals from the SLP, the BSP

Empire and Revolution

and the ILP held factory gate meetings across Clydeside, connecting the wage claim to the bigger question of capitalism and the war.

Lord Weir was an arms magnate who owned Weirs of Cathcart. He was also the government's Scottish Director of Munitions. When he brought in American experts to impose new methods and speed up production at his Cathcart munitions plant, 2,000 workers walked out. At the core of the strike were shop stewards elected from each section. Harry McShane recalled that, "The Works Committee were anti-war and had a big influence in the factory, so that men who were against the Kaiser weren't antagonistic to socialists like me who opposed the war".[127] Within four days 10,000 workers from 26 different factories were out in support and demanding the two pence an hour rise.

Arthur McManus, another of the shop stewards at Weir's, commented: "The one fact that struck home was the necessity of the workers doing for themselves what the officials were too cowardly to attempt".[128] The strike was illegal but the bosses and the government were afraid to use the law. Instead they tried divide and rule. Despite being deprived of official support and branded as "traitors" by the government and the press, the strikers stayed solid.

They set up a "Labour Withholding Committee"—a strike committee linking stewards from all the different plants across the city. They stayed out for weeks against the union officials. The city-wide strike committee eventually organised a united return to work to assert its own authority. Although they won only a limited increase, a new kind of organisation had emerged. The strike had strengthened the rank and file and fanned the flame of resistance.

In the next few months the employers tried to break shop floor control, using the new government legislation against shop stewards in three of the key munitions plants. Some stewards were threatened with the sack, some were fined and some were sentenced to three months in jail. The threat of widespread unofficial strike action saw all charges dropped and the stewards reinstated.

On the back of these victories the city wide shop stewards organisation re-established itself as the Clyde Workers' Committee (CWC). Thereafter 300 or so delegates met every weekend in Glasgow—the vast majority being stewards in engineering and the shipyards. Apart from the secretary James Messer and Davy Kirkwood, both of whom were in the ILP, all its other leading members were revolutionaries belonging to the SLP or the BSP.

John Maclean was not an elected member of the committee—he was a socialist primary school teacher, not an engineering worker. But such was his standing that he and his closest supporters were allowed to attend its meetings and participate in its debates. Indeed it is doubtful that the leaders of the CWC would have taken the lead in industrial matters had it not been for the efforts of Maclean to show that the war served only imperialist interests and should be opposed by the workers.

The CWC was not an alternative to the trade unions nor was it set up in opposition to them. It originated in the failure of the national union Executives and District Committees to place themselves at the head of the militancy of a section of the Clydeside engineers. The militants learned that if the Munitions Act was to be opposed root and branch it must be opposed by an organisation and a leadership able to act independently of the official trade union structures.

The February 1915 strike had taught them that to be effective, this organisation had to be a delegate organisation based directly in the factories. Out of their own experience the militants formulated and expressed, for the first time, the very principle of independent rank and file organisation.

Empire and Revolution

The attitude to the trade union bureaucracy was succinctly expressed in the Committee's first leaflet produced in November 1915:

> We will support the officials just so long as they rightly represent the workers, but we will act independently immediately they misrepresent them. Being composed of delegates from every shop and untrammelled by obsolete rule of law, we claim to represent the true feeling of the workers. We can act immediately according to the merits of the case and the desire of the rank and file.[129]

The CWC provided the model that militant workers across Britain would follow in the course of the war. It laid the basis for independent rank and file organisation within the existing trade unions.

A year later in 1916 the CWC would be split on the question of dilution and defeated by the government. Some of its leaders were jailed along with John Maclean, while others were deported from Clydeside, throwing the organisation into abeyance for over a year.

But later in 1916 and throughout 1917, the same kind of shop stewards' organisations sprang up in the other industrial centres—Sheffield, Barrow, Manchester, the East Midlands, London and Belfast. The Sheffield Workers' Committee was even stronger than the Clyde organisation had been in 1915. The CWC revived in 1917 and in the battles that lay ahead, the shop stewards and their new organisations would play a key role.

In 1915 resistance also spread to the South Wales coalfield, a stronghold of trade union militancy in the pre-war period. In July 1915, 200,000 miners led by revolutionary syndicalists struck for a wage increase. Again the strike was declared illegal under the Munitions Act but such was the level of solidarity that after five days the government was humiliated and forced to cave in, granting all of the miners' demands. 1915 also saw a successful wages strike of 7,000 London Transport workers.

The Glasgow rent strike of 1915

On Clydeside agitation against rent increases accompanied the industrial unrest throughout 1915. With the outbreak of war house building ceased and workers flooded into Glasgow to work in munitions. Landlords raised the rents and applied for eviction orders against tenants who couldn't pay. The hardest hit were the elderly, the unemployed and soldiers' wives—but rent rises made it difficult for even those with jobs to meet the landlords' demands.

Campaigns were initiated by local working class women, who formed tenants committees and housing associations. Some of the leading activists, like Helen Crawfurd and Mary Barbour, were members of the ILP and the local ILP councillors were demanding a rent freeze and municipal housing.

John Maclean urged the BSP and other groups to work together on the issue, even though they had fundamental disagreements with the ILP. While its leaders looked to parliament for change Maclean believed the rent struggle raised the question of working class power. In the event, his distinctive contribution to the campaign was decisive. He connected the anger over rents with the unrest in the factories and campaigned for strike action across the Clyde, using the factory gate agitation that he had developed in the prelude to the engineering strikes earlier that year.

In May 1915 the first rent strike began when tenants refused to pay increases. Rents in Govan, a key shipyard and engineering district, were increased by between 12 and 23 percent. In April the eviction of the family of a young soldier serving on the Western Front led to an angry mass protest. It was organised by Mary Barbour, a local housewife who was active in the ILP and married to an engineering worker.

Willie Gallacher recalls:

In Govan Mrs Barbour became the leader of a movement such as never has been seen before or since, for that matter…every method was used to bring the local women out and organise them for struggle. Notices were printed by the thousand and put up in the windows; wherever you went you could see them. In street after street, there was scarcely a window without one: WE ARE NOT PAYING INCREASED RENT.[130]

By August the rent strike had spread throughout the city and in September a crowd of 2,000 prevented the eviction of one of the rent strike leaders in Partick. By October 30,000 Glasgow tenants were withholding rents and the strike was spreading across Scotland and to England and Wales.

Miners at West Calder near Edinburgh struck when the mine owners tried to raise the rents of the tied housing. The strike forced the owners to back down. Throughout Glasgow there were big local demonstrations against the Sherriff Officers (bailiffs) every time they attempted an eviction and it was armies of women who stopped them:

> The women in each tenement close organised guards on a rota system. The guard on duty carried a hand bell, a racket such as used to be favoured by football fans, a tin basin and spoon—anything that would make enough noise to warn the approach of a stranger. Summoned by this noise the housewives would hasten to the scene, armed for combat. The favourite weapons were small bags filled with dry flour or whiting.
>
> The Sherriff Officers did not relish assaults with such weapons. Tenants were organised into street groups, which liaised with local Tenants' Defence Leagues, the local Women's Housing Association, the Trades Council, the Clyde Workers' Committee and the ILP councillors. By these means information could be passed on quickly and masses of people brought to a central point, for a meeting or a march.[131]

In October a tremendous demonstration in central Glasgow called on the government to curb the racketeer landlords. The government was reluctant to act but promised a Committee of Enquiry. But on Wednesday 17 November strike action brought matters to a head. On that day 18 munitions workers had been summoned to the court for non-payment of rent in an attempt by the landlords to have their wages deducted at source.

SLP member Tom Bell described how Mary Barbour's army was instrumental in what happened that day: "The women marched in a body to the shipyard and got the men to leave work and join them in a demonstration to the court". As a result all the workers from five different ship-yards downed tools and marched to the court in solidarity with all those on rent strike. "On their way from Govan one contingent marched to the school where John Maclean, already under notice of dismissal from Govan School Board, was teaching. He was taken out and carried shoulder high through the streets to the court".[132]

They were joined by delegations from all the major workplaces and by thousands of tenants. Maclean addressed the crowds outside the court. Speaking on behalf of the strikers he made it clear there would be no return to work until the charges were dropped. The demonstration also agreed that he should telegram Prime Minister Asquith stating, "This demonstration of Clyde munitions workers requests the government to state not later than Saturday that it forbids any rent increase during the period of the war. Failing this, a general strike will be called on Monday, November 22nd".[133]

The Sheriff persuaded the landlord to drop the cases and telephoned the cabinet. Scared of the consequences of a strike spreading throughout the munitions indus-try, the government promised it would introduce a Rent Restriction Act, tying rents all over Britain to the pre-war level. The victory of the rent strike is a highpoint in British working class history, and brought Maclean to the attention of a wider audience.

The BSP newspaper *Justice* was controlled by Hyndman and the pro-war faction of the party. In late 1915 Maclean launched *The Vanguard* as the paper of the Glasgow BSP, which held a clear anti-war position. In *The Vanguard* Maclean emphasised the powerful position now held by many workers—for a political strike to stop the war: "Capitalism, that is the right to rob the creators of wealth, must be killed and it can be done in twelve solid months, starting any time, if but the workers are ready".[134]

The limitations of trade unionism

It was from the revolutionary groups to the left of the ILP that the CWC drew its leadership—the British Socialist Party and the Socialist Labour Party. But the revolutionaries were influenced by industrial unionism and tended to separate politics and economics. Their reluctance to raise wider political issues on the shop floor for fear of dividing the rank and file was a big obstacle.

All of them were active against the war but as Maclean argued, "they were inclined to leave their politics at the factory gate". He knew this would make it easier for the government to isolate and break the movement. In December 1915 Maclean and his supporters were expelled from CWC meetings for demanding it call action against the war.

Harry McShane, a young shop steward at Weir's of Cathcart at the time, sided with Maclean:

We had read about the mass political strikes in Russia before the war and we knew Luxemburg's "The Mass Strike". But in Britain the next struggle was against dilution—a very difficult fight for socialists who had always been opposed to craft trade unionism and advocated industrial unions. The CWC led the struggle against dilution, and John Maclean fell out with the leaders. He was opposed to the way the socialists on the committee were behaving. I agreed with him. John argued that the main struggle was against the war. Most of the stewards were anti-war socialists, but they had submerged their politics in workshop struggles—not mentioning the war inside the factories.

Willie Gallacher's conduct in particular angered Maclean. At the end of 1915 Willie came to speak at Bath Street, where the meetings were at the centre of our anti-war fight. He did not mention the war at all. Maclean criticised him openly, asking, "How could any man calling himself a socialist speak at a meeting and not refer to the war that is raging in Europe?"[135]

Maclean was proved right. While the ILP presence on the CWC was small, the revolutionaries failed to build an effective political alternative to it with disastrous results. In the spring of 1916 this weakness allowed the government and the bosses to suppress the CWC and impose dilution.

They were assisted by Davy Kirkwood, ILP convenor at Beardmore's huge munitions plant at Parkhead Forge, and his mentor John Wheatley, ILP councillor for Shettleston, who would later become an MP and Minister for Health in the first Labour government. Together they collaborated with Lloyd George's Dilution Commissioners to undermine the CWC.

The reformist ILP faction on the CWC, represented by Davy Kirkwood, argued for a negotiated dilution settlement. Kirkwood's proposal had been drawn up behind the scenes along with ILP councillor Wheatley. The rest of the CWC were unaware of this and the fact that the Dilution Commissioners on the Clyde were sympathetic to the ILP proposal.

Empire and Revolution

Lloyd George comes to Glasgow

Events moved quickly as the government took the initiative. Lloyd George came to Glasgow, hoping to win over the rank and file. He planned to tour the key workplaces and negotiate a breakthrough on dilution. But his visit turned into a personal humiliation. The CWC stewards refused to negotiate with him on a piecemeal, plant by plant basis. However, Kirkwood ignored the CWC stand and met Lloyd George at Parkhead Forge to discuss the ILP proposals. The following day Lloyd George met the rest of the CWC and no agreement was reached.

He then addressed a monster rally of engineering workers in the huge St Andrews Concert Hall in Glasgow on Christmas Day, not then a holiday in Scotland. But his attempt to bypass the shop stewards failed and he was shouted down in a protest organised by the CWC. When he left the hall it was to a chorus of the "Red Flag". Reports of Lloyd George's reception were censored. But Maclean ignored the ban and reported it in *The Vanguard*: "Seldom has a prominent politician, a leading representative of the governing classes, been treated with so little respect".[136]

However, the cabinet had made contingency plans to deal with matters should Lloyd George's overtures fail; they now brought these into play. The offensive was co-ordinated by Sir William Weir, the arms magnate. As yet the Red Clydesiders had built few links with the rest of the country. The government exploited this weakness to isolate the shop stewards and impose dilution on the Clyde.

Lloyd George knew that taking immediate action against the leading members of the CWC would provoke a mass strike so they started with safer targets. The Russian refugee and comrade of Maclean's Peter Petroff and his wife were interned under the Defence of the Realm Act in January 1916. *Forward*, the mildly left-wing ILP newspaper, was raided and banned for a brief period. Maclean's *Vanguard*, which sold 3,000 copies a week in Glasgow, was seized and never appeared again during the war. Maclean was arrested in February on charges of sedition. In the same month police raided the SLP offices and smashed the printing presses of the CWC newspaper, *The Worker*.

In the week Maclean was arrested a unilateral dilution agreement was signed between the Dilution Commissioners and Kirkwood on behalf of the workforce at Parkhead Forge. This broke the common front of the CWC and its failure to act encouraged the government to step up its repression. Three of its leaders, including Willie Gallacher, were arrested and charged with sedition. Initially they were refused bail but when 10,000 munitions workers stopped work, they were released until their trial.

At this point Beardmore's management, with the prior approval of the cabinet, reneged on its side of the deal with Kirkwood. When Kirkwood tried to encourage the first group of women who arrived at Parkhead under the new dilution agreement to join the union, management banned him from speaking to the women's section and revoked the shop stewards' right of access to other areas of the plant. This threatened to curtail effective union organisation in the biggest factory on the Clyde.

The Parkhead workers struck in protest and were followed by mass walkouts at Weir's, North British Diesel Engines and at Beardmore's other plant in Clydebank. But the hostility to Kirkwood's "go it alone" moves on dilution made it hard to spread the action—particularly in the absence of a call from the CWC.

While the question of solidarity hung in the balance the government rounded up the key leaders of the CWC. Kirkwood and the leading stewards at Parkhead Forge and Arthur McManus and leading militants at Weir's were arrested and deported from Glasgow. The press was banned under the Defence of the Realm Act from reporting the arrests and deportations. Despite Kirkwood's moderation, he was too prominent to ignore; the government was out to break reformist trade union resistance to the war economy, as well as the revolutionary opposition to the war itself.

At this point, had the CWC called a co-ordinated stoppage against the dilution agreement and against the deportations it could have inflicted a serious defeat on the government and re-asserted its authority. A motion calling for an all-out strike was actually proposed at a CWC meeting but the chairman, Willie Gallacher, ruled it out of order.

The trials involving the "Clydeside Reds" took place in Edinburgh during April and May. Maclean appeared first to face six charges, including incitement to strike against conscription and for inciting soldiers to mutiny. The judge, Lord Strathclyde, imposed a savage sentence of three years' penal servitude. Maclean would remain in prison until June 1917 when, under the impact of the Russian Revolution, mass working class protest forced his release. Jack Smith, shop stewards' convenor at Weir's, got an 18 month sentence. Gallacher, Jimmy Maxton of the ILP and James MacDougall, Maclean's right hand man, were sentenced to a year. The other CWC members were either deported from Glasgow or jailed for three months. The government refused to make any concessions on dilution to the CWC, even refusing to meet a deputation. The repression robbed Clydeside of its leadership and Maclean was silenced for two years. Militancy subsided and resistance to dilution collapsed.

The smashing of the Clyde Workers' Committee was a terrible blow but it was not final. The events reverberated throughout the factories and made an indelible impression on thousands of workers who had previously been indifferent to politics. While the struggle on the Clyde was put into temporary abeyance, resistance soon spread to other munitions centres.

In 1922 Kirkwood was elected to Westminster as one of the "Red Clydeside" group of MPs. Later he was elevated to the House of Lords. In his autobiography he described why, in December 1915, he broke ranks with the CWC:

> We were all scared as the thundering masses of Germans tramped their way towards the coasts. That night I went to John Wheatley. In thirty minutes he drafted the scheme, which became the basis for the whole of Britain and worked perfectly till the end of the war...the extremists attacked us for having agreed increased production. John Maclean made me the theme of innumerable speeches.[137]

Kirkwood and Wheatley sabotaged the Clyde Workers' Committee. Unlike John Maclean, none of the ILP leaders believed in striking to stop the war. Kirkwood's autobiography is titled *My Life of Revolt*. Harry McShane always insisted it should have been called "My Revolting Life".

Sheffield and the struggle against conscription
Lloyd George's victory over the shop stewards' movement saw him promoted from Munitions Minister to Secretary of State for War in the National Government. In 1916 he had no qualms about ordering the execution of James Connolly and the other leaders of the Dublin Rising.

It was Lloyd George who imposed conscription to ensure the smooth flow of cannon fodder to the front. He ordered the Battle of the Somme in which over a million were slaughtered and admitted he was playing the role of "the butcher's boy". At the end of 1916 he engineered Tory support for a cabinet coup to oust Asquith and make himself prime minister. But while the arrogant Lloyd George wallowed in bloodshed, revulsion to the war grew.

The Sheffield Workers' Committee was built out of successful unofficial action against conscription. In October 1916 Leonard Hargreaves, a fitter working at the Vickers munitions plant was conscripted despite a government pledge not to draft skilled munitions workers. After the horrors of the Somme, conscription was like a death sentence, yet the leaders of Hargreaves's union refused to act.

Sheffield shop stewards, led by J T Murphy, an SLP member who worked at Vickers, organised mass meetings to demand that Hargreaves be returned to civilian life. When the authorities refused, the shop stewards moved fast and 12,000 Sheffield engineers walked out on strike. Motorcycle delegations were sent out across the country to win support for the strike. Within three days the action had spread to other centres and the government caved in. As a result shop stewards organisation was established throughout Sheffield and a new scheme was established exempting skilled munitions workers from military service.

The Easter Rising

Ireland was Britain's oldest colony and in Dublin on Easter Monday 1916 the first serious revolt against the war took place. For over a century two traditions had dominated the opposition to British rule: constitutional nationalism, which sought limited Home Rule through the British parliament; and republicanism, committed to an armed rebellion to drive out the British.

To date neither had been successful. By the summer of 1914 the unionist campaign and their threat of civil war had convinced the Irish Home Rule Party that even the creation of one Irish parliament under the British crown was impossible. As the party of the southern Irish landowners and capitalists, they reached an agreement with their Anglo-Irish, unionist counterparts in July 1914.

Ireland was to be partitioned north and south. Excluded from the Home Rule settlement were the six north-eastern counties—the area that contained the greatest concentration of industry and where a unionist majority prevailed.

However, a month after the partition deal was agreed, the First World War started and Home Rule was put on ice.

The constitutional nationalists rushed to support the British war effort and helped persuade thousands of Irishmen to volunteer for the slaughter. In return they were promised Home Rule after the war, provided they accepted partition. It was a betrayal that led to a rapid growth in militant republicanism.

On Easter Monday 2,000 armed rebels seized control of the General Post Office and other key public buildings in central Dublin. Most of those taking part were radical republicans, led by the poet, Padraic Pearse. Alongside them fought a smaller contingent from the Irish Citizen Army, an organisation formed during the Dublin Lockout of 1913 to defend the strikers. Made up of Dublin trade unionists, socialists and left-wing republicans, it was led by James Connolly, the founder of Irish socialism and organiser of the Irish Transport & General Workers' Union.

Connolly knew the partition of Ireland would be disastrous because it would secure the rule of the bosses and lead to what he predicted would become "a carnival of reaction, north and south". But his perspective was not a purely Irish one. He was determined to strike a blow for Irish freedom but he believed that against the backdrop of the First World War, a revolt in Dublin was bound to have worldwide significance.

Ireland was close to the heart of the greatest imperial power and a blow struck in Dublin would encourage the struggle of colonial people throughout the empire. In weakening the biggest empire in the world an Irish rebellion could start a chain reaction against the war and against imperialism: "Ireland may yet set a torch to a European conflagration that will not burn out until the last throne and the last capitalist bond and debenture will be shrivelled on the funeral pyre of the last warlord".[138]

Unfortunately the organisation of the rising was botched. The commander of a key group countermanded the order to mobilise and the numbers that took part were reduced by two thirds. The insurgents numbered less than 3,000 men and women and the rising was crushed after six days by 10,000 British troops and naval bombardment from battleships in the mouth of the Liffey.

The population of Dublin seemed to react with indifference, while the left, including most of the revolutionary left, were shocked at Connolly's involvement and dismissed the rising as an attempted putsch. John Maclean, who was imprisoned by the British state only two weeks beforehand, was one of the few British socialists to defend the rising and Connolly's involvement. Maclean's pamphlet, *The Irish Tragedy—Scotland's Disgrace*, attacks the blatant hypocrisy of an imperialist ruling class that claimed to be defending democracy in Belgium while crushing it in Ireland.

Trotsky, writing for the Russian journal *Nashe Slovo*, pointed out: "Scottish soldiers smashed the Dublin barricades but in Scotland itself miners are rallying round the red banner raised by John Maclean".[139]

Lenin saw the Easter Rising as the first blow against the war and British imperialism. He defended the rising by pointing out: "It is the misfortune of the Irish that they rose prematurely before the European revolt of the working class had had time to mature".[140]

Within two years that would change. The brutal measures taken by the British ruling class to crush the Easter rebellion—the destruction of central Dublin by naval bombardment and the execution of 15 of its leaders after they had surrendered—deepened the animosity to continuing British rule. When the British tried to introduce conscription in Ireland it provoked widespread opposition. Sinn Fein won a landslide victory in the general election at the end of 1918, with the Unionists even losing half their seats in Ulster. Sinn

Fein refused to take their seats at Westminster, disavowing Britain's right to rule Ireland. Instead they met in Dublin to proclaim the new Irish Republic. Ireland was headed for its war of independence.

10

From war to revolution

"The imperialist war is ushering in the era of social revolution. All the objective conditions of recent times have put the workers' revolutionary mass struggle on the order of the day. It is the duty of socialists, while making every use of every means of the working class's legal struggle, to develop the workers' revolutionary consciousness, promote and encourage any revolutionary action, and do everything possible to turn the imperialist war between peoples into a civil war for the conquest of political power by the working class and the realisation of socialism".

—*Resolution of the Zimmerwald Left, September 1915.*[141]

When Karl Liebknecht voted against German war credits in the Reichstag in December 1914 he became the bitter enemy of the right-wing social democrats, but according to a begrudging Karl Kautsky, it also made him "the most popular man in the trenches".[142]

By the summer of 1915 disaffection with the war was growing and the Bolsheviks sought to build the revolutionary opposition to it on an international basis. At first it had seemed that the war had split the socialist movement into two parts—the "social patriots", who supported their own governments and who were the great majority, and the internationalists.

It soon became clear that the movement was really split in three because the internationalists were themselves divided between consistent revolutionaries and what became known as the "centre". The centrists adopted a pacifist or semi-pacifist position and were in favour of a negotiated peace. They wanted to rebuild links between the various socialist parties and looked back to a rebirth of the old International rather than the building of a new one. Duncan Hallas writes:

> They saw the war as a disastrous interruption of "normal" life, not as an opportunity for the socialist revolution. For them the International was for "peacetime". For May Day speeches, not for revolutionary struggle to change the world.[143]

Towards a new International

Lenin believed the war could create the basis for a new International and that the Bolsheviks had to fight for that position. In a letter to the Bolshevik factory worker Alexander Shlyapnikov he wrote: "Our task is now an absolute and open struggle with opportunism. This is an international task. It rests upon us, for there is no one else. We cannot put it aside".[144]

In September 1915 38 delegates from 11 countries gathered at a conference of anti-war socialists held at Zimmerwald, near Berne in Switzerland. The conference had been convened by the Italian and Swiss socialist parties. Both were dominated by the centre and wanted to restore the International as a "force for peace". The delegates joked among themselves that 50 years after the founding of the First International it was possible to seat all the internationalists in four coaches.

At Zimmerwald the split between the centrists and the revolutionary left was brought into the open. Lenin argued for a break with the Second International, insisting that maintaining links with its right-wing leadership would disarm the working class. The conference rejected by 19 votes to 12 Lenin's draft resolution, which argued to turn imperialist war into civil war. In spite of this Lenin saw the conference

Empire and Revolution

as a first step and the left, including the Bolsheviks, voted for the majority position as well as publishing their own rejected resolution.

Lenin explained why: "It is a fact that this manifesto is a step towards a real struggle against opportunism, towards a rupture with it". Despite its "timidity and inconsistency, it would be sectarian to refuse to take this step forward".[145]

And now Liebknecht's was no longer a lone voice, even in the German Reichstag. In December 1915 19 other deputies had joined him in opposing the war credits. Zimmerwald was making an impact.

At the BSP Easter conference in 1916, the pro-war Hyndman leadership was decisively beaten and forced out of the party. The new leadership adopted a centrist, pacifist position but the imprisoned John Maclean, who shared Lenin's revolutionary opposition to the war, was elected to the BSP executive for the first time and a campaign was launched for his release.

The follow up to Zimmerwald was held at Kienthal in Switzerland in April 1916. This conference took place against the backdrop of the continuing slaughter at Verdun. It was another step towards Lenin's position—the necessity of mass struggle in ending the violence of imperialism. Lenin was calling for a political break, not only with the right, but also with the fake left—those who supported pacifism and saw negotiations between the warring powers as the way to end the war. In the period between the Kienthal conference and the February Revolution of 1917 the left gained ground.

Lenin could now look to groups in Germany, France, Britain, the Netherlands, Sweden, Bulgaria and Italy who agreed on the need to break from the Second International. "In every significant national movement a left radical faction aligned with Lenin's position had come into being. The Zimmerwald left tendency was well on the way to becoming a movement".[146]

Karl Liebknecht and Otto Rühle, elected Reichstag deputies, had broken with the SPD and were agitating against the war. The SPD membership fell by 63 percent between 1914 and 1916 and its national conference was torn apart by dissension over its support for the war.

Karl Liebknecht was on the far left of the SPD and, along with Rosa Luxemburg, was a member of the Spartacus League, a network of revolutionaries working within the SPD. Paul Mason describes the impact of his speeches:

In April 1916 Oskar Hippe came to Berlin to work alongside his brother-in-law in a munitions factory. The factory had 100 percent union membership. "On the eve of 1 May 1916 my brother-in-law told me we would not go to work the next day, since the workforce would all be joining an anti-war demonstration on the Potsdam Platz. We went there at the specified time. Ten thousand workers had gathered in the square and Karl Liebknecht spoke to them from the platform of the Potsdam local station." Liebknecht had been called up for military service and then expelled from the SPD in January 1916. As a serving soldier he knew what he was about to say would land him in jail but he also knew its impact would be massive. The crowd marched out of the factories in silence, telling bystanders "Keep your tongue between your teeth" in symbolic protest at press censorship of Liebknecht's speeches.

Liebknecht told them: "The poor, unfortunate German soldier...the sufferings he endures are past description. About him everywhere shells and bombs sow death and destruction. His wife and children at home and suffering want and hardship; she looks about her and finds her children crying for bread...everyone must keep his or her tongue between their teeth, for the war profiteers must make money out of the want and misery of the wives and their husband soldiers at the front." As the crowd cheered him he shouted

"Do not shout for me, shout 'We will have no more war. We will have peace now!'" At this point the police attacked. As the demonstration was dispersed Liebknecht was arrested but the street fighting continued into the evening.[147]

On the day of his trial, 55,000 Berlin workers struck in solidarity with him.

His May Day speech, his trial and imprisonment and the strike that it provoked opened up a much deeper rift in the SPD. So it was that a centrist current developed in opposition to its pro-war leadership. The centre and left groupings—including the Spartacus League—would be expelled from the SPD in January 1917 and would come together to form the Independent Social Democratic Party (USPD) in the spring of 1917 on a centrist anti-war programme.

1917: the turning point

1917 marked the fundamental turning point in the First World War. By the end of 1916 Russia's backward peasant economy and its archaic state structure led it to collapse under the pressure of the war. The mass of the people were suffering and in the first weeks of 1917 St Petersburg saw strikes, lock-outs and long queues for inadequate supplies of flour.

By 1917 a number of countries were close to breaking point. The Russian Revolution that began in February was the most spectacular expression of a Europe-wide crisis that shook all the warring nations. It was led by women textile workers agitating over bread shortages on International Women's Day.[148] It was a remarkable movement which began a process of transformation in the land and the people involved.

Revolutions change people in quite astonishing ways. They are so astonishing that they are often hard to believe. We live in regimented worlds, with the limits of change constantly before us. Moments of radicalisation—strikes, demonstrations, and popular protests—can give us an inkling of the changes that can occur. But then we are pulled back into the world we know.

But revolutions, and especially great revolutions, involve seismic shifts. They involve sustained mobilisations that require a real leap of the imagination to understand. The result is both inspirational and discomforting. Such was the revolution that began on 23 February, 1917.[149]

The Tsar, who days before had seemed all-powerful, abdicated on the morning of 2 March. By November a revolutionary government headed by Lenin was running the country.

No one expected a revolution on 23 February, not even Lenin and the Bolsheviks. It was International Working Women's Day, a tradition established in 1910 by the German socialist Clara Zetkin. The underground socialist groups in St Petersburg were planning to mark the day with meetings, speeches and leafleting.

War weariness had fuelled massive anger and February had seen the introduction of food rationing. But because tensions had been running high, most of the experienced socialists did not feel the time was ripe for militant action. When they heard the women in the textile plants were planning a strike some were aghast, while others were at best lukewarm and cautioned against it. "Not a single organisation called for strikes on that day", recalled Trotsky in his *History of the Russian Revolution*. "What is more, even a Bolshevik organisation, and the most militant one—the Vyborg District Committee, all workers—was opposing strikes". On the day the left-wing organisations were more positive, though many were still not convinced. "'Once there is a mass strike, one must call everybody on to the streets and take the lead', said Vasilii Kayurov, a Bolshevik who encouraged this response".[150]

But it was the "leaders" who were running to catch up with "led". The women textile workers of St Petersburg were by no means the vanguard of the class under normal circumstances. But their bitterness at the terrible bread shortages, and many with husbands at the front, was such that they went on strike on their own initiative. 90,000 came out onto the streets of St Petersburg to show their anger and to demand change. And they dragged the Bolshevik metalworkers of the Vyborg district behind them.

An engineering worker from the Nobel factory recalls the mood among the women textile workers:

> We could hear their voices: "Down with hunger! Bread for the workers!" Masses of women workers in a militant frame of mind filled the lane. Those who caught sight of us began to wave their arms, shouting, "Come out! Stop work!" Snowballs flew in through the windows. We joined the revolution.[151]

The government brought out its most reliable troops—the feared Cossack cavalry. They did not mutiny but they did not do what was expected of them either:

> The Cossacks charged repeatedly but without ferocity... the mass of demonstrators parted to let them through and closed up again. There was no fear in the crowd. The Cossacks' promise not to shoot was passed from mouth to mouth...but towards the police the crowd showed massive hatred...28 policemen were killed.[152]

The next day the movement involved half of St Petersburg's 400,000 factory workers and the slogans had changed from "Bread" to "Down with the autocracy! Down with the war!" The government tried to break up the protests by using armed police and regiments waiting to go to the front. But on the fourth day of strikes and demonstrations, mutiny swept through the army barracks and workers and soldiers intermingled and marched through the streets with red flags and guns, arresting the police and government officials. Regiments sent to the city to restore order went over to the side of the revolution. Railway workers refused to allow the movement of troops.

Similar events swept Moscow and the other major cities. As the rank and file of the army switched allegiance, the Tsarist monarchy, which had celebrated its 300th anniversary in 1913, collapsed. The Tsar's generals warned him they would not be able to restore order unless he abdicated. On 2 March he did so. Casualties in the February days were considerable. 433 were killed and 1,214 wounded. The Tsar's police had fired on the crowds and some of the policemen and other figures of authority were killed or beaten in retaliation. But the new Russia was born in jubilation, as Mike Haynes writes:

> The old authorities collapsed and ecstatic crowds joined symbolic marches or enormous public meetings to mark the change... One of the new socialist papers noted that the "the yellow press calls itself non-party socialist...while the banks try to protect themselves by raising the red banner of the revolution over their buildings".
>
> It is an image worth pausing on as a measure of the change. You wake up one morning and see the most reactionary newspapers proclaiming some sort of allegiance to socialism, even though it is not your socialism... And above you see, over the impressive banks, monuments to the stability of the system, red flags fluttering in the wind.[153]

Two bodies emerged to take on the functions of government. One, the provisional government, was based among the bourgeois politicians in the old state Duma, overwhelmingly on the side of the landowners, the businessmen and the generals. It was immediately recognised by the Allies,

Empire and Revolution

concerned to keep Russia in the war. The provisional government was initially headed by a representative of the monarchy, Prince Lvov, and consisted mostly of industrialists. But it was also joined by Alexander Kerensky, a member of the workers' and peasants' Social Revolutionary party. He became Prime Minister in July.

The other body that emerged was made up of workers' delegates, drawn together in the workers' councils, modelled on the soviet that the St Petersburg workers created in the 1905 revolution.

The key question was which of these bodies would take power. Either the Russian capitalist class would move to crush the workers' councils or the councils would take power.

As Megan Trudell explains, this was an unstable situation pregnant with potential:

> Their revolution as yet still hadn't overcome the contradictions of capitalism... The idea of fighting a war for democracy and liberty fitted well with the sentiments of overthrowing the Tsar. But the act of ridding Russia of its monarchy gave people a sense of how society can be changed, and when the Provisional Government refused to stop the war that was creating hardship it failed to stop the momentum for revolutionary change.[154]

The impact of the February Revolution on Britain

The February Revolution inspired massive peace demonstrations in Britain, Germany, Italy and Austro-Hungary. In March 1917, 12,000 packed into the Albert Hall in London to support the Russian Revolution. Another 5,000 supporters couldn't get in.

The mood of optimism lifted the industrial struggle. Although five million workers had been mobilised in the armed forces Britain's trade union membership was growing and strikes increasing. A general revival in working class confidence was taking place and this was boosted by news of the February Revolution.

In March 10,000 munitions workers took strike action in Barrow and in May the largest unofficial strike movement of the war began in Rochdale—a strike to prevent the extension of dilution to commercial contracts and to defend the scheme exempting skilled workers from military service. It spread rapidly throughout the Manchester area and then to Sheffield, Rotherham and Coventry. Eventually 48 towns and cities were affected and over 200,000 workers were involved. The government responded by arresting the strike leaders and a compromise agreement was reached.

As a result of all this action the National Shop Stewards' and Workers' Committee Movement was launched and it established a National Advisory Council (NAC) to act as reporting centre for the movement up and down the country. But the NAC, as its name implied, held no executive power. This was no accident. Most of the leaders of the shop stewards' movement opposed the idea of centralised national leadership and insisted on local autonomy.

Localism was allied to a deep-rooted sectionalism, and it would bedevil the movement in the battles to come.

On May Day 70,000 marched through Glasgow in solidarity with the February Revolution. At the end of May another demonstration of 90,000 marched to Glasgow Green to protest against Lloyd George being granted the freedom of the city and to demand the release from prison of John Maclean and Peter Petroff, a hero of the 1905 Russian Revolution. Two hundred Russian sailors left their warship as it lay at anchor on the Clyde to join this march. In June the All Russian Congress of Workers' and Soldiers' Deputies sent their fraternal greetings to "the brave fighter for the International, comrade Maclean and expresses their hopes that the new rise of international solidarity will bring his liberty".[155] Maclean was released later that month.

Empire and Revolution

In September 1917 Lenin wrote:

> There can be no doubt that the end of September marked
> the beginning of a new period in the history of the Russian
> Revolution and, very probably, of the world revolution.
> The world working class revolution was first begun with
> engagements by isolated combatants, representing with
> unequalled courage, all the honest elements of "official"
> socialism—Liebknecht in Germany, Adler in Austria,
> Maclean in England [sic]; such are the best known of these
> isolated heroes who assumed the heavy task of precursors of
> the revolution.[156]

That's why Liebknecht, Adler and Maclean were elected,
along with Lenin, Trotsky and Spirodinova, as honorary
presidents of the first All-Russian Congress of Soviets and
why, at the beginning of 1918, Maclean was appointed the
Bolsheviks' Official Consul in Glasgow.

Mutinies and desertions

Throughout 1917 there were mutinies and mass desertions in
the French, Russian, British, Italian, Austrian, Turkish and
German armies. In October 1917 the Italian army was badly
defeated at the battle of Caporetto. The enemy commander,
Erwin Rommel, described the Italian soldiers' response to
his invitation to surrender:

> Suddenly the mass began to move and in the ensuing panic
> swept its resisting officers downhill. Most of the soldiers
> threw their weapons away and hurried towards me... An
> Italian officer who hesitated to surrender was shot down by
> his own troops. For the Italians on Mrzli peak the war was
> over. They shouted with joy.[157]

Despite attempts by the provisional government to run
the war "efficiently", two million Russian soldiers deserted
between February and October 1917.[158] In 1917 the number of

sick rose rapidly and so did requests for home leave. Sabotage at the front began to take place on a wider scale and on parts of the Eastern Front during Easter 1917 there was fraternisation between the troops similar to that seen on the Western Front during Christmas 1914.

In June a major offensive, using the best units of the Russian army, was launched in an attempt to turn the tide. 40,000 were killed and after an initial advance the collapse intensified. "Authority and obedience no longer exist. For hundreds of miles one can see lines of deserters, armed and unarmed, in good health and in high spirits, certain they will not be punished".[159]

Still the provisional government remained committed to war, driving both soldiers and sailors towards the Bolshevik slogan—"Down with the War!" The figures showing the growing influence of the Bolshevik agitators in the Russian armed forces speak for themselves:

> The total number of Bolsheviks in the army at the time of the February revolution was a couple of thousand. By the time of the April Conference it had risen to 6,000 and on 16 June it was 26,000. After that, soldiers in practically all corps, divisions and other units began to join the party. On 5 October, on the north-western front alone there were 48,994 party members.[160]

Bolshevik influence spread throughout the army and beyond it. The Russian army, like the population at large, was predominantly peasant. Partly through the influence of the Bolshevik soldier-agitators the peasants were drawn into the revolution and the provisional government became increasingly paralysed.

Germany 1917

The toppling of the Tsar and the collapse of Russia's military machine sunk the SPD right-wing's feeble excuse that it

Empire and Revolution

was "a war for national defence against Russian tyranny". To a growing minority of German workers the real menace was the war policy of the German state.

By 1917 real wages had fallen across industries. Food was so scarce that the German winter of 1916-17 became the "turnip winter". In April militants who opposed the war led a strike of 200,000 Berlin workers against a further reduction in bread rations.

Like those on Clydeside and in Sheffield, the revolutionary shop stewards filled the vacuum created by the union officials. The war gave Berlin's 300 munitions plants tremendous bargaining power. The dramatic rise in inflation meant the shop stewards were called upon to mount a constant defence of living standards. The first two years of the war saw real wages in Germany's munitions industry fall by only 22 percent compared to a 42 percent drop in the rest of the economy.

The mass of Berlin workers did not immediately reject the war but they were ready to fight against its economic impact. According to Richard Müller, senior shop steward in the DWM munitions factory, the rank and file leaders were "solid union men who reflected the better traditions of the pre-war labour movement. As shop stewards on the lowest rung of the union machine, they had virtually the unlimited trust of a great section of workers".[161]

Despite press censorship, the workers became aware of two important events—the February Revolution in Russia and news of demonstrations in Leipzig by women demanding bread. The Berlin shop stewards decided it was time to lead a stoppage against the war but the police aimed to pre-empt it by arresting their leader, Richard Müller.

Yet three days later Berlin was paralysed as 200,000 workers came out on strike and were joined by engineering workers in other cities. On 16 April the Leipzig bread protest escalated into a political challenge to the state. Strikes erupted and Leipzig produced the first German workers' council.

As well as demanding bread, it made political demands—for peace without annexations; the abolition of the labour laws; the end of censorship and freedom for political prisoners. In Berlin the 10,000-strong workforce at DWM elected a factory council of three workers and three USPD members. Three other local factories followed suit and for a time it looked like the shop stewards' initiative would transform the strike from a food protest into a challenge to the war.

But in 1917 the Prussian state machine was still intact. Police arrested the key militants, the factories were placed under martial law and the strikers began drifting back to work. Müller's arrest had weakened organisation and the union officials were able to step in and defuse the unrest.

In April 1917 the Independent Social Democratic Party of Germany (USPD) had been launched on an anti-war programme. Its leaders were 20 left-wing Reichstag deputies, including the SPD Reichstag leader of 1914, Hugo Haase, and the theoretician Karl Kautsky. Its core activists were the revolutionary shop stewards, and it also included Karl Liebknecht, Rosa Luxemburg and the group of revolutionaries around them in the Spartacus League.

Six months after its launch, the USPD could claim 120,000 members as against the 150,000 in the SPD. Many of the strike leaders of April 1917 and the forthcoming January 1918 mass strikes were in its ranks. However, "the split was forced by the SPD right-wing, the anti-war platform was pacifist, not revolutionary. The USPD was a mish-mash of reformists, centrists and some revolutionaries. It reflected the growing opposition to the war among German workers; it did not lead it".[162]

Spontaneous revolt over food shortages led to political opposition to the war itself. The summer of 1917 saw the spirit of rebellion spread to the German fleet, which sheltered in the ports of the north-west coast, its commanders afraid of confrontation at sea with the British navy. As the war had dragged on, the class divide had become more apparent, as Chris Harman writes:

> The difference in the living conditions between the officers and the men was emphasised by their close proximity on the ships. The crew saw that their superiors ate better food, went ashore when they pleased and had special clubs for their entertainment. Resentment gave way to organisation as food rations were cut. The sailors felt they could build something akin to trade union organisation, and there were hunger strikes and work stoppages demanding recognition for such committees.

But in August the authorities arrested a number of sailors. The crew on one ship took protest action, only to abandon it. Their passive trade union approach was impotent against the armed might of the state and its military "justice". The movement collapsed and two of its leaders were executed; others were sentenced to hard labour. "The sailors learnt a bitter lesson; you cannot take on a military machine with peaceful 'non-political' protests. They were to remember all this 14 months later".[163]

Italy 1917
Even before the October Revolution militant workers in Turin knew about Lenin and the Bolsheviks. News of the February Revolution and the overthrow of the Tsar brought widespread hope to Italian workers that the February events would go further and bring an end to the war.

On May Day 1917 anti-war demonstrations led by women and young people were held in the northern cities. They continued over the early summer and reached their peak in Turin. A delegation from the Russian provisional government came to the city in August to address a mass rally of 40,000 munitions workers. The Russians were there to urge their Italian brothers and sisters to help them produce more weapons. They were astonished to be repeatedly heckled as large sections of the crowd kept chanting "Viva Lenin!"

Two weeks later the city was gripped by food riots. They were reminiscent of the February strikes in St Petersburg and the Leipzig strikes in April, in that they were initiated by working class women. The women were expected not only to queue for hours for meagre rations of food but also to work a 12-hour day in the factories. What started as bread riots turned into insurrection as the women made links with other groups of workers.

On 21 August eight of the city's bakeries failed to open and women and children demonstrated across the city to demand bread. Workers at the Diatto-Frejus factory began demonstrating outside the factory gates, chanting "We haven't eaten. We can't work. Give us bread!" Management came out and promised they would order bread if they would immediately return to work. In response the workforce started shouting "To hell with the bread! We want peace! Down with the profiteers! Down with the war!"[164] They stayed out on strike. On 24 August angry crowds converged in the centre of Turin and were driven back by tanks and machine guns. Four days of rioting followed and at the end of it 50 demonstrators were dead and 800 jailed.

Others were arrested and sent to the frontline units in the trenches.

For all its intensity, the August riot had only begun to tap the collective power of the organised workers. A wind of revolt had blown through Turin but when it subsided the only evidence of its passing were the corpses. Without organisation, no amount of self-sacrifice and courage could overcome the military power of the state. Physical confrontation having failed, action in the factories would acquire new importance.[165]

Empire and Revolution

The 1915 strike against Italy's declaration of war, the 1917 bread riots and the new surge of self-organisation in the factories had all shown how much the city's working class opposed their rulers and their bloody war. These wartime struggles laid the basis for the Turin factory council movement that emerged as the war ended. The old order on the land was under threat too. Peasant conscripts and landless labourers were returning from the trenches with a hatred of the officer class and a burning sense of injustice against those who had sent them to war. The news from Russia was that the revolution was giving the land to the people who worked on it.

II

The Russian Revolution

"The one party to see a clear way forward was the Bolsheviks. Their perspectives began to be crystallised in April 1917, when Lenin returned from exile and argued that the party should not support the Provisional Government. It should stand on the most radical wing of soviet democracy under the slogan 'All power to the soviets'. The leaders of the other socialist parties were horrified. So too were some Bolsheviks. But these arguments struck a chord with many existing members and attracted new ones".[166]

In February mass strikes and demonstrations by the workers of St Petersburg had overthrown the Tsar. Eight months later a revolutionary workers' party was able to win a majority of the workers', soldiers' and sailors' councils, brush aside the weak provisional government and take power.

In the months between February and October it is estimated that the Bolsheviks grew from 20,000 members to over 300,000. Within the factories, workers' committees spontaneously formed from February onwards and by October there were over 2,000 of them. The most advanced were in St Petersburg where there were over 120.

Factories had already formed their own Red Guards. Under the leadership of the Bolsheviks they mobilised in late August to defeat the attempt by General Kornilov's counter-revolutionary forces to overthrow the provisional government, replace it with a military dictatorship and restore the monarchy.

By October there were over 150,000 Red Guards across

Russia. Rank and file committees also appeared in the army and navy. In April 100,000 sailors, based at Kronstadt, Tallinn and Helsinki elected their Baltic Fleet Committee. Its chairman was the Bolshevik sailor Pavel Dybenko.

But the highest forms of organisation in all this activity were the "soviets" or councils that spread across the whole of Russia, binging together elected delegates from the workplaces and all the various committees. The old order was collapsing and something new was emerging from below to replace it. By May there were 400 soviets in Russia; by August 600 and by October 900. The most developed was the St Petersburg soviet, the first to emerge out of the February Revolution. With 3,000 delegates, a pedigree from the 1905 Revolution and an executive committee that met day to day, the St Petersburg soviet had the moral authority to lead. As in 1905 its chair was Leon Trotsky.

In June, when the first All Russian Congress of Soviets of Workers' and Soldiers' Deputies had met (there was a separate congress for peasant soviets), the Bolsheviks were in a minority. When the Second Congress met in October it was bigger, and the majority of delegates were revolutionary. With 505 out of 670 delegates voting for the resolution on "All Power to the Soviets", the Bolsheviks led the victorious insurrection and took power on 25 October.

Compared with the February Revolution it was virtually bloodless with only 15 casualties. Support for the provisional government had simply melted away.

> "Understand, please", said Martov, Menshevik leader and opponent of the insurrection, "what we have before us after all is a victorious uprising of the proletariat—almost the entire proletariat supports Lenin and expects its social liberation from the uprising".[167]

When Lenin addressed the Congress of Soviets at its meeting on the day after the uprising, his opening words were, "We shall now proceed to construct the socialist order".[168] And by 8 November the new workers' government was in place: "The task for which the people have been struggling is assured—the immediate offer of a democratic peace, the abolition of the landed property of the landlords, worker control over production and the creation of a soviet government".[169]

The Bolsheviks offered an immediate armistice to all the powers at war with Russia, pending a permanent peace based on no annexations and no indemnities. They made public all the secret treaties and machinations behind the war: "The Bolsheviks published the secret agreements on war aims reached between the Entente powers: Britain, France and Italy stood convicted...of annexationist ambitions comparable with those of the monster which they were pledged to extirpate, German Militarism".[170]

To underline the point, the Bolsheviks renounced Tsarist Russia's colonial possessions. The workers' government badly needed peace—it would be the key to delivering bread and land—but its leaders knew imperial Germany would not accept peace on the terms offered. German capital had gone to war not to "defend German culture", as the majority of the SPD leadership believed or pretended to believe, but to grab territory and economic advantage. However, the Bolsheviks reckoned their appeal for peace would turn people throughout the world, and especially in Germany, against their own governments. "If none of the states will accept an armistice...we shall be able to call this war just and defensive... Russia will become the ally of the world proletariat, of all the oppressed of the globe".[171]

By the end of 1917 workers across Europe were clamouring for peace and ready to fight for a better world. Having led the revolution to success in Russia, the Bolsheviks set about spreading it. They began by producing *The Torch*, a paper for distribution to the German soldiers in the trenches along the Eastern Front. Half a million copies of each issue were printed and distributed.

The German High Command saw the Russian peace offer as a chance to expand the German Empire and sent representatives to negotiate with the Bolsheviks at the town of Brest Litovsk, where they demanded a huge area of the former Tsarist Empire and reparations. But the Russian negotiators were appealing as much to the German workers and soldiers as to their generals and politicians:

> When Trotsky arrived at Brest Litovsk in December 1917, he was accompanied by the Polish-Austrian who had been an active revolutionary in Germany before the war, Karl Radek. Radek, before the eyes of the diplomats and officials assembled on the railway platform to greet them, began to distribute pamphlets among the German soldiers. The negotiations broke down in the face of German demands for annexations and revolutionary Russia had to sit back helpless as German troops advanced.[172]

News of the Bolshevik peace offer and Germany's rejection angered all those fed up with the war in Germany and Austro-Hungary. Many militants agreed with what Karl Liebknecht wrote from prison:

> Thanks to the Russian delegates Bresk-Litovsk has become a revolutionary platform with reverberations felt far and wide. It has denounced the central European powers. It has exposed the German spirit of brigandage, lying, cunning and hypocrisy. It has delivered a crushing judgement on the peace policy of the German Majority, a policy which is not so much hypocritical as cynical.[173]

In the first few weeks of 1918 the Spartacus League issued mass leaflets calling for a German general strike over the question of peace, while the more moderate USPD opponents of the war called for a three-day strike. But this agitation was superseded by news of momentous events in the neighbouring Austro-Hungarian Empire.

Mass strikes rock the Central Powers

At the beginning of January mass strikes swept Vienna and Budapest; strikes not for money but for peace. On 14 January the workers at the Daimler works in the Austrian town of Wiener Neustadt on the outskirts of Vienna struck against a cut in the food ration. At the same time workers in the Csepsel munitions works near Budapest, the biggest munitions factory in Hungary, walked out. The strike spread rapidly, as Chris Harman writes:

> Within two days all the factories throughout both cities were closed. The Austrian Socialist Party estimated a quarter of a million workers were on strike in the Vienna region alone. Nor was that all. In Vienna workers' councils were elected and their demands were: the abolition of censorship; the end of martial law; the eight-hour working day; and the release of imprisoned anti-war socialist Friedrich Adler.
>
> ...It was the biggest protest anywhere yet against the effects of the war. It did not take long for what had happened in German-speaking Austria to reverberate in Berlin. The Spartacus League there put out a leaflet telling how "the Viennese workers elected councils on the Russian model" and proclaiming "Monday 28 January the beginning of the general strike in Germany".[174]

The call was taken up by the revolutionary shop stewards' leader Richard Müller and the Berlin munitions workers followed suit. 400,000 workers struck and were joined the next day by another 100,000. The movement spread way beyond the confines of Berlin, involving Kiel, Hamburg, Danzig, Magdeburg, Nuremburg, Munich, Cologne, Mannheim, Kassel and the Ruhr. Nowhere had the official leadership called the strike, yet the movement shook the Central

Powers to their very foundations with more than two million workers involved.

Over 400 factory delegates met in Berlin and appointed an action committee. The workers' council that grew from this struggle was a model of organisation, with one delegate elected for every 1,000 workers. The programme they adopted linked their economic demands with the demand that the German government immediately accept the Bolshevik peace proposals.

Yet despite the massive revolutionary potential the movement was contained. Like the big mutinies in the French army in 1917 or the Kiel sailors of the previous summer, it lacked a coherent revolutionary leadership. The strikers were inspired by the Russian Revolution yet the Berlin workers still had enough illusions in the pro-war SPD leaders Ebert and Scheidemann to hand them places on the action committee and they used that influence to undermine the strike and ensure its defeat.

> The militants had not given much thought as to what to do once it was successful. As one of the Spartakist leaders wrote shortly afterwards, "they did not know what to do with the revolutionary energy".
>
> In order to establish the unity of the whole working class in the strike, the action committee had insisted, against some opposition, on representatives from the pro-war SPD joining the Committee.[175]

But the SPD politicians were only prepared to join for one reason, as Ebert explained several years later: "I entered the strike leadership with the firmly determined intention of bringing the strike to an end as soon as possible and in this way saving the country from disaster".[176]

Ebert even defied the law by speaking at a banned meeting, but only to damage the movement in a way that the authorities could never have done themselves: "It is the duty of the workers to back up their brothers and fathers at the front and to manufacture the best arms... Victory is the dearest goal of all Germans".[177]

The Social Democrat leaders misled the action committee by offering to mediate with the government, but only over the economic demands. The strike leadership were unhappy but had no clear alternative. They recognised the war was the crucial issue even although they had used economic questions to mobilise the workers. But to end the war needed revolutionary action as well as strikes. Leo Jogiches summed up the problem:

> Because they could not imagine the strike wave as more than a simple protest movement, the committee, under the influence of the Reichstag deputies, tried to enter into negotiations with the government instead of refusing all negotiations and directing the energy of the masses.[178]

The SPD and USPD politicians abandoned the strike committee, leaving the revolutionary shop stewards with the choice of armed insurrection or retreat. When the SPD threw all its weight into ending the strike, the tremendous solidarity began to wane. Judging the moment premature for insurrection, the shop stewards backed down and on 3 February the strike ended.

In the resulting demoralisation the government seized their opportunity. Many of the strike leaders were arrested and in Berlin one worker in ten was sent to the front. Like the Kiel sailors in the summer of 1917, the strike was beaten because it tried to use trade union tactics to deal with the problem of political and military power.

In spite of this defeat, the notion of workers' councils was firmly established among the best workers. At first some of the Spartacists were dubious about this new institution but by the summer of 1918 they had decided that "the coming revolution must place all power in the hands of the workers'

Empire and Revolution

councils, the organised power of the proletarian masses, as in Russia".[179]

The Russian working class was around five million. The German working class was ten times bigger. Yet in February 1917 the Bolsheviks had 20,000 cadres, while in the summer of 1918 there were probably only 3,000 revolutionaries in the whole of Germany—and they had to contend with the treacherous leaders of the SPD. They were not well organised. "They had no united organisation, no tradition of working within a common discipline, no way of arriving at an agreed strategy or tactics, no method for selecting from among themselves leaders who were reliable and had cool heads. Yet these revolutionaries were about to enter one of the most intense periods of class struggle in the history of capitalism".[180]

Britain: strike action against the war

In January 1918, while mass strikes were sweeping the Central Powers, the leadership of the shop stewards movement at last decided to call for a national strike to force the British government to start peace negotiations. A number of factors encouraged them: the impact of the October Revolution, the stalemate on the Western Front, and the acute food shortage at home—in Manchester 100,000 workers marched against food shortages.

Despite a big campaign and huge meetings of engineering workers threatening strike action, the national strike did not materialise. At the last moment the leaders of the skilled engineers drew back from their political challenge to the state, opting instead for a militant but highly sectional demand for the continued exemption of skilled workers from military conscription.

The shop stewards movement had developed between 1915 and 1918, when the big issue affecting everyone was the war. Yet, with few exceptions, the stewards were reluctant to raise the issue of a political opposition to the war inside the factories for fear of losing support, even though many of them were anti-war and anti-capitalist themselves. JT Murphy was one of the key leaders of the movement. In 1917 he wrote the famous pamphlet of the shop stewards movement, *The Workers' Committee*, but it never even mentioned the war.

The engineering workers could have been the vanguard of a struggle to end the war and challenge British capitalism; alas their power was never fully marshalled for this purpose on a national basis.

On 5 January the leaders of the shop stewards movement met in Manchester and demanded that "the government accept the invitation of the Russian government to consider peace terms".[181] In Glasgow, where Maclean had consistently denounced the war, the call was taken up with enthusiasm. At the end of January a huge meeting in Glasgow supported the CWC's call for a strike against the war.

But in the key districts of Sheffield and Manchester workshop meetings voted against the demand. The national body failed to give a lead and at that point Glasgow did not feel strong enough to act alone. The problem was localism and the absence of real national leadership. In February 1918 the National Advisory Committee of the Shop Stewards and Workers Committee Movement published its position: "If we could only be certain that the German workers would follow suit, we would have no hesitation in calling for an immediate policy of down tools and damn the consequences. But we are not in touch with our fellow workers in Germany. It may be that they are willing to do the bidding of their warlords".[182]

The tragedy is they were unaware that workers in Austro-Hungary and Germany had just launched illegal mass strikes against the war involving over two million workers.

John Maclean believed that if the national shop stewards body wouldn't lead on the war, then the Clyde should.

Empire and Revolution

Three months later, on May Day, workers in Glasgow struck for peace.

Ever since his release from prison the previous June Maclean had been agitating for action against the war and urging support for the Russian Revolution. In January he was appointed Bolshevik Consul and spoke at meetings across the UK, arguing the best defence of Russia was revolution in Britain. The cabinet was concerned about the political situation on the Clyde and Maclean's influence.

The Ministry of Munitions Clyde Labour report for week ending 15 December commented: "The early months of 1918 may reveal industrial action with a view to the achievement of political ends in the termination of war conditions". At a riotous meeting between the Clyde shop stewards and the government conscription minister, Auckland Geddes, in January 1918, they demanded a negotiated peace and expressed support for the initiatives of the soviet government. By then the shipyards were on strike and for that month the Clyde contributed three quarters of all strike days lost.

The Minister of Munitions put the blame squarely on "the pacifist and revolutionary section of men", warning "if the trouble on the Clyde continues, it may have grave results of which the country should be made aware". By January 1918 the demand for increased wages was coupled with a call for peace, which explicitly challenged the nature of the war and the class character of the government. On 2 February the situation was described as "grave" and a "stoppage of work on a large scale extremely probable".

The Ministry of Labour highlighted Beardmore's as a possible flashpoint. "From the evidence before the Industrial Commissioner's department it is clear that bad relations exist. The dangerous fact is that Gallacher, McManus and one or two more of the most powerful extremists are employed at Beardmore's in various works. That they have the will and power to exploit trouble can be shown by the serious consequences threatened by the alleged victimisation of four women workers where a national strike was suggested". The Ministry urged the Prime Minister to intervene directly otherwise "Beardmore's might provide the spark which lights a big fire".[183]

In early 1918 local anti-war public meetings several thousand-strong were being held by the BSP and the ILP, while Maclean's Marxist classes were attracting up to 1,000 workers a week. Reports in *Forward* and the BSP's *Call* show that national Labour leaders like Ramsay MacDonald had to pay lip service to Lenin's peace policy when they were speaking to Glasgow audiences. There was also strong pressure from the ILP rank and file throughout Clydeside for Labour to oppose the war.[184]

In February, as a result of Munitions Ministry concerns about industrial unrest, the General Officer of the Army in Scotland asked the Cabinet to "arrange" another prosecution against Maclean. The authorities wanted him silenced. In early April he had been speaking at public meetings in the Durham coalfield and had just returned to Glasgow when he was arrested and charged with sedition. He was refused bail and held at Duke Street prison in Glasgow pending his trial, which was set for 9 May at the High Court in Edinburgh.

The Glasgow May Day Committee decided to hold its annual demonstration on a working day, Wednesday 1 May, and to call for a stoppage against the war. It was a tremendous show of working class solidarity, with a mass strike and a march to the jail where Maclean was awaiting trial:

Glasgow Trades Council and the other union organisations on their May Day Committee had been won to support a stoppage and detailed work secured a massive response. Few estimates put the number attending below 90,000 and despite a heavy police presence no attempt was made to stop the march. Resolutions were passed in favour of a cessation of hostilities, the release of Maclean and support for the Russian Revolution.[185]

MacLean was brought to trial on 9 May. He used the dock of the High Court in Edinburgh as a platform to speak out against the capitalist system, ending with an appeal to the working class to overthrow it:

No government is going to take from me my right to protest against wrong... I am not here as the accused, I am here as the accuser of capitalism, dripping with blood from head to foot... Fifteen years from the end of this war we are into the next war if capitalism lasts; we can't escape it... My appeal is to the working class...because they, and they alone, can bring about the time when the whole world will be in one brotherhood, on a sound economic foundation... That can only be obtained when the people of the world get the world and retain the world.[186]

The judge sentenced Maclean to five years' penal servitude and immediately there was a massive campaign for his release.

Lenin, in his speech to the Russian Trade Union Congress, said: "The British government imprisoned him because he exposed the object of the war and spoke out against the criminal nature of British imperialism—and this time not only as a Scottish schoolteacher, but also as the consul of the Soviet Republic".[187]

Russia and the outcome at Brest Litovsk
The Bolsheviks had never supposed it possible to build socialism in an isolated Russia and as Lenin insisted again in January 1918: "Without the German revolution we are ruined".[188] Trotsky, in charge of the Soviet delegation at

Brest Litovsk, tried to stall and buy time for a German revolution to come to Russia's aid. But the defeat of the massive strike wave in February had delayed revolution in Germany and the prospect of an immediate break-up of the German army.

Ignoring the Bolsheviks' peace offer at Brest Litovsk, the German generals ordered their troops to advance into Russia. There were arguments throughout the Bolshevik party and the soviets about what to do. Bukharin and others argued for a revolutionary war against Germany. In the end Lenin persuaded most of the others that accepting the German ultimatum was the only realistic option.

Like Lenin, Trotsky was always clear about the impossibility of such a revolutionary war. In January he said: "We had to delay the negotiations as long as we could but it is clear as day, that if we wage revolutionary war we will be overthrown".[189] Peace negotiations were resumed on 1 March and the peace treaty with Germany was signed on 3 March, with the Soviet delegates making it clear they were signing under duress. Before signing they issued the following statement:

> Under the circumstances Russia has no freedom of choice. The German proletariat is as yet not strong enough to stop the attack of German Imperialism. We have no doubt that the triumph of imperialism and militarism over the international proletarian revolution will prove temporary. Meanwhile the Soviet government, unable to resist the armed offensive of German Imperialism, is forced to accept peace terms to save revolutionary Russia.[190]

The terms were punitive. Russia lost a quarter of its territory and 44 percent of its population, one third of its crops, 27 percent of its state income, 73 percent of its iron and 75 percent of its coal.[191] Rosa Luxemburg, imprisoned at Breslau, had foreseen the dangers of the Russian Revolution

Empire and Revolution

being isolated and had written to Karl Kautsky's wife, Luise, about it at the end of November 1917:

> Are you happy about the Russians? Of course they won't be able to maintain themselves in this witches' Sabbath, not because statistics show economic development in Russia to be too backward, as your clever husband has figured out, but because social democracy in the highly developed West consists of miserable, wretched cowards who will look on and let the Russians bleed to death.[192]

12

The German Revolution and the end of the war

"The First World War precipitated an international revolutionary crisis. That the climax had already occurred in the Bolshevik Revolution of October 1917 was far from apparent during the immediate post-war years. October was widely seen, both on the right and on the left, as a beginning, not an end. Reasonable men could anticipate the Hungarian, Austrian, German, Italian, French and even the British revolutions. In particular it was the form of the soviet, of Workers' Councils, that characterised the international crisis".[193]

By March 1918 the German ruling class was confident that with the anti-war strike movement quelled and with Russia now out of the war, the military could concentrate all its forces on the unfinished business on the Western Front. "It was possible for one contemporary writer on the split inside the SPD to claim in May that the effect of peace in the East had been to 'draw the masses to the side of the government'."[194]

With the imminent arrival of large numbers of American troops on the Western Front, the German High Command knew they would have to secure victory against the British and the French during the spring of 1918. But they were confident of doing so, for the military odds had shifted in Germany's favour. Serbia, Romania and Russia were already defeated.

Without an active Eastern Front, the basis of the alliance's strategy became meaningless. For the first time since August 1914 the Central Powers were free to concentrate all their efforts in the West... Those who could envisage the war ending in the coming year could do so only on the basis of a German victory.[195]

This was the view of the German High Command in March 1918, when they launched a series of offensives on the Western Front. At first big advances were made and it looked as if the British were facing defeat as they struggled to cope with the German onslaught. But the massive spring offensive stretched German resources beyond breaking point.

Their offensive ran short of food, supplies and men and it failed to make the expected breakthrough. As their initial gains were rolled back by an Allied counter-offensive—now reinforced by US troops—the German High Command began to see the possibility of defeat. After the military setbacks at the battle of the Marne in late September, they were completely panicked. Just months earlier they had been discussing the possibility of imposing a Brest Litovsk on the British and French. The debate inside the German ruling class had not been whether war or peace, but how much could be annexed after a German victory. Now Ludendorff realised that the whole front would collapse unless Germany could be quickly extricated from the war.

Desertion and desperation

Masses of German soldiers and workers had already begun to see the sense of Karl Liebknecht's anti-war slogan, "The main enemy is at home". Mass desertions and stay-aways by army conscripts and reservists had seriously reduced the offensive capacity of the German army during 1918. The collapse began after the halting of the spring offensive. Later Ludendorff admitted that influenza, the potato famine at home and a shortage of 70,000 recruits per month had caused seven army divisions to break up, at least one of which "absolutely refused to fight". With the breakdown in morale came a change in political attitudes. One officer told Ludendorff that "he thought he had Russian Bolsheviks under him, not German soldiers".

Ludendorff complained that "the loss by desertion was uncommonly high. The number that got into neutral countries ran into tens of thousands and a far greater number lived happily at home, tacitly tolerated by their fellow citizens and completely unmolested by the authorities".[196] As we saw in Chapter 7, it is estimated that from mid-1917 to the end of the war more than two million German soldiers deserted.

Hindenburg and Ludendorff held an emergency meeting with the Kaiser at the end of September. They told him the war was lost and the situation was desperate; that an immediate negotiated peace was the only hope of avoiding a complete collapse and a terrible defeat. They also advised him that "the only way to guarantee social stability was to replace their own absolute power by that of a new, liberalised government, including Social Democratic ministers":

> The Kaiser was astounded. The Prussian military elite were suggesting its traditional enemy be brought into the government. They insisted there was no choice. As the secretary of state, Hinze, put it: "it is necessary to prevent upheaval from below by revolution from above". So with the blessing of the most illiberal sector of German society, a "liberal" coalition government was formed. The Chancellor was the Kaiser's cousin, Prince Max of Baden. Its programme—concessions, both to the German workers and to the Allied powers. Its aim—to save the monarchy.

One of the basic principles of the SPD had always been republicanism. Now the party leaders agreed to join a

Empire and Revolution

government whose reason for existence was to preserve the monarchy. The party secretary, Ebert, told a meeting of its leadership: "If we don't come to an understanding with the bourgeois parties then we will have to let events take their course... A similar development would take place to that experienced in Russia". That was enough to convince his colleagues that it was right to support the efforts of Prince Max—but it was too late for such support to lay the spectre of revolution.[197]

Talk of armistice had a dramatic impact on an already disintegrating army as desertions, mutinies and a reluctance to fight spread like wildfire. "In the last weeks of the war German deserters at the front and on the lines of communication were highly organised, with a level of political consciousness and organisation that enabled them to overthrow the German military government in Belgium".[198]

It also created new opportunities for the forces on the left. The feeling that the political regime was in turmoil gave workers confidence to fight and demonstrate on the streets. In October Liebknecht was released from jail but the concession was not enough to dampen the growing unrest. The major grievance was the war, and despite the talk of armistice it was still not over.

The German High Command had hoped for an acceptable compromise in peace negotiations but the Allies, notably France, were determined to do unto Germany what Germany had done to Russia—destroy its military strength, grab its territory, share out its colonies and loot its economy.

At first the German ruling class could not stomach such savage "reparations" and preferred to urge its increasingly reluctant army to fight on, for what was a lost cause. It was now certain Germany would lose the war, yet while the Kaiser was pleading for "peace with honour", the naval high command ordered the fleet out to sea on a suicide foray against the British navy. It was a desperate gamble to change the odds but when the sailors at Wilhelmshaven were ordered to move their ships at the end of October, they responded by putting out the ships boilers.

"As one sailor wrote to his father, 'We all felt this would be our last voyage and so we refused to follow orders'".[199] They were arrested but the movement was not crushed as it had been a year before. Five days later thousands of sailors marched through Kiel to protest at the arrests and were joined by the port's workers. The German Revolution had begun.

> In November 1918 the "bodies of armed men", which, as Engels had pointed out, are the essential core of a state machine, began to turn on their masters. "By 4 November revolutionary feeling in Kiel was at fever heat", wrote the historian of the German Revolution. "The High Command and the officers of the navy surrendered, while some on the battleship Koenig and other vessels were killed. The sailors had become masters of the situation and the army units in the area joined them.
>
> "In Kiel there was only one authority—the council of workers', soldiers' and sailors' deputies... From Kiel the rebellion spread to Hamburg and on the night of 8 November it was learned in Berlin that it had triumphed, with little or no resistance, in Hanover, Magdeburg, Cologne, Munich, Stuttgart, Frankfurt am Main, Brunswick, Oldenburg, Wittenburg and other cities... At 8am on 9 November the general strike broke out in Berlin itself".[200]

Revolution in Berlin

The call for the Berlin general strike was answered in all of the factories. An especially reliable front line unit—the Kaiser Alexander Regiment—was rushed to Berlin to put down the uprising. It mutinied and joined the revolution. The Kaiser fled to Holland. The German workers, through

the war did the Spartacus League finally form
Communist Party. It proved too late to be deci-
tive.[202]

he revolution started at the end of October
artacus League had only 3,000 members. Peter
his biography of Rosa Luxemburg, reveals its
ngs:

ationally Spartakus was slow to develop. In the most
nt cities it evolved only in the course of December
many cases not until February and March of 1919.
pts to arrange caucus meetings of Spartakist sympa-
within the Berlin Workers' and Soldiers' Council
ot produce results and an independent Communist
s within the Berlin council was only formed on 20
uary 1919.[203]

ntime the struggle between revolution and counter-
ion was approaching its climax, with the creation of
ctive combat party long overdue. Rosa Luxemburg at
latedly decided on this course but only after her call for
ial USPD conference had been rejected by the USPD
rship, who were afraid of providing the Spartacists with
pportunity of winning more support.

tween 30 December 1918 and 1 January 1919, 112 del-
es from different parts of Germany came together in
attempt to tackle this glaring deficiency by turning the
rtacus League and its sympathisers into an independent
rman Communist Party (KPD). The Left Radicals in the
PD held a simultaneous conference and decided to join
e newly formed KPD forthwith.

But throughout the KPD founding conference there was a
arked contrast in the understanding of the dynamics of the
tuation between the older leaders and a majority of the del-
gates. The most important question was whether or not the

their councils of deputies, found themselves in power. Huge
crowds of workers and soldiers carrying guns and red flags
thronged the streets of Berlin.

The revolutionary shop stewards and the Spartacists, a
persecuted minority only weeks before, now had the support of tens of thousands. Karl Liebknecht, recently released
from prison, led a column of soldiers and workers to seize
the imperial palace. He proclaimed "the socialist republic
and the world revolution" from its balcony window. The
Armistice was signed two days later on 11 November and the
war was finally over—ended by the German Revolution.

But while the workers and soldiers were taking over the
city, the SPD leaders were in talks with the leaders of the old
regime. Prince Max handed the premiership to Ebert, the
SPD leader, in an attempt to stabilise the situation. A "joint
revolutionary government" was formed of three members of
each of the two Social Democrat parties but with the SPD
clearly in control. It was given a revolutionary veneer and
called the "council of people's commissars". In reality it was
set up by the moderates as a way to "save" Germany from a
socialist revolution along Russian lines.

> In fact it was far from revolutionary—the three SPD mem-
> bers had, a mere 24 hours earlier, been frantically trying
> to stop the revolution. Only one of the so-called commis-
> sars, Emil Barth, came from the left. Liebknecht had been
> offered a place in this "revolutionary government" but
> refused, knowing he would be a prisoner of the non-revo-
> lutionary majority... Barth was not so principled. But the
> revolutionary veneer was good enough to fool the workers
> and soldiers—at least for a few vital weeks.

The "revolutionary government" was formed on 10
November, the second day of the revolution in Berlin. The
Spartacists and the Left Independents had made their own
preparations for solving the question of power that day.

They called for an assembly of workers' and soldiers' deputies—one delegate for each 1,000 workers and for each battalion of soldiers.

But when the assembly convened, the revolutionaries found matters rather different from what they had expected. The SPD leaders had put their party machine to work to ensure their dominance at the assembly. The previous day, while the revolution was raging, they had set up their own soldiers' and workers' councils, made up of half a dozen hand-picked Social Democrat workers and three of the party leaders. They then rushed thousands of leaflets to the army barracks demanding "no fratricidal strife".

The politically raw soldiers were given the impression that anyone who questioned the need for unthinking unity between the different "socialist" parties was a splitter, wrecker and saboteur. 1,500 delegates packed out the meeting hall and it was difficult for left-wing workers' delegates to object when SPD notables took charge of the platform.

The soldiers were not happy and started heckling, especially when Liebknecht put a question mark over the revolutionary euphoria, warning them, "The counter-revolution is already underway. It is already in action. It is already among us". His warning had no effect on the soldiers. They insisted on putting 12 SPD soldiers on the executive for the Workers' and Soldiers' Council of Berlin—alongside 12 workers—six of whom came from each of the Social Democrat parties.[201]

Effectively the organ of revolution was now controlled by those who feared and opposed the revolution. The German councils had given power to men determined not to use it for revolutionary ends. This was clearly shown when the executive voted to relinquish its sovereignty to a Reichstag that would be elected on 19 January—a parliamentary National Assembly for which the classes opposed

to the revolution would ⌐
had made it.

After the October Revo⌐
persed the Constituent Asse⌐
to the soviet of workers', so⌐
After the November Revolutic⌐
the soviets in favour of the N⌐
of the Bolsheviks' action was t⌐
effect of the SPD's action in G⌐
the bourgeois state.

The betrayal of the revolution⌐
and the Independents (USPD) w⌐
the new Prime Minister, was on⌐
Groener of the military high com⌐
Workers' and Soldiers' Assembly. A⌐
the wartime dictator, they agreed to⌐
order in the army, so they could re⌐
at large. By "order" they meant a ret⌐
tures of repression and ruling class pow⌐
ripped asunder.

The launch of the German Communist ⌐

Tony Cliff in his political biography of R⌐
underlines the lateness of her break⌐
Luxemburg had helped form the Spartacu⌐
faction inside the SPD. But she and the Spa⌐
stayed with Kautsky when he and others sp⌐
SPD to form the Independent Social-democrat⌐
USPD, in April 1917.

This was despite the fact that the USPD was a⌐
liamentary party, pacifist in its attitude and as C⌐
out, opposed to mass strikes and demonstration⌐
the war. Only with the outbreak of the Germar⌐
tion and the eruption of workers' and soldiers' cou⌐

the end of⌐
Germany'⌐
sively effe⌐

When ⌐
1918 the S⌐
Nettl, in ⌐
shortcomi⌐

Organi⌐
import⌐
and in⌐
Attem⌐
thiser⌐
did n⌐
cauc⌐
Febr⌐

Me⌐
revolu⌐
an eff⌐
last b⌐
a spe⌐
leade⌐
an o⌐

B⌐
ega⌐
an ⌐
Sp⌐
G⌐
U⌐
th⌐

new party should contest the National assembly elections.

Luxemburg argued in favour. Although the purpose of the National Assembly would be to consolidate the power of the new bourgeois regime, she maintained that because the majority of workers were still in favour of the National Assembly elections, socialists had to contest the elections and fight within the Assembly. This was not in order to win mere reforms under capitalism, but "to utilise the platform of the National Assembly itself to denounce mercilessly all its wily tricks, to expose its counter-revolutionary work step by step to the masses, and to appeal to them to intervene".[204]

The other leaders were in agreement but the great majority of delegates at the conference voted to boycott the elections and the National Assembly. This majority was so certain of the victory of the German Revolution that it thought participation in parliamentary elections was a diversion. In vain Luxemburg warned the delegates of underestimating the difficulties that lay ahead; of counting on a quick, easy victory; and against neglecting a great opportunity for winning new adherents and a new audience.

The next day, in introducing the session on the new party programme, she went to great lengths to stress that the revolution was still in its early stages:

It was characteristic of the early days that the revolution remained exclusively political—the first stage of a revolution whose main tasks lie in the economic field. It is the very essence of this revolution that strikes become the central focus. It then becomes an economic revolution and therefore a socialist revolution. The struggle for socialism has to be fought out by the masses, in every factory, by every proletarian against their employer. Only then will it become a socialist revolution.

Socialism will not and cannot be created by decrees; nor can it be established by any government, however socialist.

Socialism must be created by the masses—where the chains of capitalism are forged, there must they be broken.

Luxemburg argued the need was to "undermine the Scheidemann-Ebert government step by step", not to try and seize power before the conditions were ripe, but to fight "in every province, in every city, in every village, in every municipality, in order to transfer all the power of the state bit by bit from the bourgeoisie to the workers' and soldiers' councils".[205]

Her powerful, passionate speech won massive applause but the majority of the delegates did not grasp the key point she was making—that the decisive conflict for state power was still some considerable distance away and that what was needed now was revolutionary patience. The majority did vote for the following statement, which should have made Rosa's position absolutely clear:

> The KPD will never take over governmental power except in response to the clear, unambiguous will of the great majority of the proletarian masses of all Germany, never except by the proletariat's conscious affirmation of the views, aims and methods of struggle of the KPD... The KPD will never enter the government just because Ebert and Scheidemann are going bankrupt and the USPD, by collaborating with them are in a blind alley.[206]

But the majority were far from patient, as the votes at conference proved. Events in the days ahead would pull the less cool-headed of the new KPD in the opposite direction and lead to catastrophe.

The conference had voted, against Luxemburg's advice, to boycott the forthcoming parliamentary elections. Luxemburg's position tallied with Lenin's. He argued that so long as workers have illusions in parliament and social democracy, revolutionaries have to participate in elections to their councils of deputies, found themselves in power. Huge crowds of workers and soldiers carrying guns and red flags thronged the streets of Berlin.

The revolutionary shop stewards and the Spartacists, a persecuted minority only weeks before, now had the support of tens of thousands. Karl Liebknecht, recently released from prison, led a column of soldiers and workers to seize the imperial palace. He proclaimed "the socialist republic and the world revolution" from its balcony window. The Armistice was signed two days later on 11 November and the war was finally over—ended by the German Revolution.

But while the workers and soldiers were taking over the city, the SPD leaders were in talks with the leaders of the old regime. Prince Max handed the premiership to Ebert, the SPD leader, in an attempt to stabilise the situation. A "joint revolutionary government" was formed of three members of each of the two Social Democrat parties but with the SPD clearly in control. It was given a revolutionary veneer and called the "council of people's commissars". In reality it was set up by the moderates as a way to "save" Germany from a socialist revolution along Russian lines.

> In fact it was far from revolutionary—the three SPD members had, a mere 24 hours earlier, been frantically trying to stop the revolution. Only one of the so-called commissars, Emil Barth, came from the left. Liebknecht had been offered a place in this "revolutionary government" but refused, knowing he would be a prisoner of the non-revolutionary majority... Barth was not so principled. But the revolutionary veneer was good enough to fool the workers and soldiers—at least for a few vital weeks.
>
> The "revolutionary government" was formed on 10 November, the second day of the revolution in Berlin. The Spartacists and the Left Independents had made their own preparations for solving the question of power that day.

They called for an assembly of workers' and soldiers' deputies—one delegate for each 1,000 workers and for each battalion of soldiers.

But when the assembly convened, the revolutionaries found matters rather different from what they had expected. The SPD leaders had put their party machine to work to ensure their dominance at the assembly. The previous day, while the revolution was raging, they had set up their own soldiers' and workers' councils, made up of half a dozen hand-picked Social Democrat workers and three of the party leaders. They then rushed thousands of leaflets to the army barracks demanding "no fratricidal strife".

The politically raw soldiers were given the impression that anyone who questioned the need for unthinking unity between the different "socialist" parties was a splitter, wrecker and saboteur. 1,500 delegates packed out the meeting hall and it was difficult for left-wing workers' delegates to object when SPD notables took charge of the platform.

The soldiers were not happy and started heckling, especially when Liebknecht put a question mark over the revolutionary euphoria, warning them, "The counter-revolution is already underway. It is already in action. It is already among us". His warning had no effect on the soldiers. They insisted on putting 12 SPD soldiers on the executive for the Workers' and Soldiers' Council of Berlin—alongside 12 workers—six of whom came from each of the Social Democrat parties.[201]

Effectively the organ of revolution was now controlled by those who feared and opposed the revolution. The German councils had given power to men determined not to use it for revolutionary ends. This was clearly shown when the executive voted to relinquish its sovereignty to a Reichstag that would be elected on 19 January—a parliamentary National Assembly for which the classes opposed to the revolution would have the same vote as those who had made it.

After the October Revolution the Bolsheviks had dispersed the Constituent Assembly and chosen to hand power to the soviet of workers', soldiers' and peasants' delegates. After the November Revolution the German SPD dissolved the soviets in favour of the National Assembly. The effect of the Bolsheviks' action was to create a workers' state; the effect of the SPD's action in Germany was to reconstitute the bourgeois state.

The betrayal of the revolution by the leaders of the SPD and the Independents (USPD) was now underway. Ebert, the new Prime Minister, was on the phone to General Groener of the military high command the day after the Workers' and Soldiers' Assembly. Along with Hindenburg, the wartime dictator, they agreed to collaborate to restore order in the army, so they could restore order in society at large. By "order" they meant a return to the old structures of repression and ruling class power that had just been ripped asunder.

The launch of the German Communist Party

Tony Cliff in his political biography of Rosa Luxemburg underlines the lateness of her break with Kautsky. Luxemburg had helped form the Spartacus League as a faction inside the SPD. But she and the Spartacus League stayed with Kautsky when he and others split from the SPD to form the Independent Social-democratic Party, the USPD, in April 1917.

This was despite the fact that the USPD was a purely parliamentary party, pacifist in its attitude and as Cliff points out, opposed to mass strikes and demonstrations against the war. Only with the outbreak of the German revolution and the eruption of workers' and soldiers' councils at the end of the war did the Spartacus League finally form Germany's Communist Party. It proved too late to be decisively effective.[202]

When the revolution started at the end of October 1918 the Spartacus League had only 3,000 members. Peter Nettl, in his biography of Rosa Luxemburg, reveals its shortcomings:

> Organisationally Spartakus was slow to develop. In the most important cities it evolved only in the course of December and in many cases not until February and March of 1919. Attempts to arrange caucus meetings of Spartakist sympathisers within the Berlin Workers' and Soldiers' Council did not produce results and an independent Communist caucus within the Berlin council was only formed on 20 February 1919.[203]

Meantime the struggle between revolution and counter-revolution was approaching its climax, with the creation of an effective combat party long overdue. Rosa Luxemburg at last belatedly decided on this course but only after her call for a special USPD conference had been rejected by the USPD leadership, who were afraid of providing the Spartacists with an opportunity of winning more support.

Between 30 December 1918 and 1 January 1919, 112 delegates from different parts of Germany came together in an attempt to tackle this glaring deficiency by turning the Spartacus League and its sympathisers into an independent German Communist Party (KPD). The Left Radicals in the USPD held a simultaneous conference and decided to join the newly formed KPD forthwith.

But throughout the KPD founding conference there was a marked contrast in the understanding of the dynamics of the situation between the older leaders and a majority of the delegates. The most important question was whether or not the new party should contest the National assembly elections.

Luxemburg argued in favour. Although the purpose of the National Assembly would be to consolidate the power of the new bourgeois regime, she maintained that because the majority of workers were still in favour of the National Assembly elections, socialists had to contest the elections and fight within the Assembly. This was not in order to win mere reforms under capitalism, but "to utilise the platform of the National Assembly itself to denounce mercilessly all its wily tricks, to expose its counter-revolutionary work step by step to the masses, and to appeal to them to intervene".[204]

The other leaders were in agreement but the great majority of delegates at the conference voted to boycott the elections and the National Assembly. This majority was so certain of the victory of the German Revolution that it thought participation in parliamentary elections was a diversion. In vain Luxemburg warned the delegates of underestimating the difficulties that lay ahead; of counting on a quick, easy victory; and against neglecting a great opportunity for winning new adherents and a new audience.

The next day, in introducing the session on the new party programme, she went to great lengths to stress that the revolution was still in its early stages:

It was characteristic of the early days that the revolution remained exclusively political—the first stage of a revolution whose main tasks lie in the economic field. It is the very essence of this revolution that strikes become the central focus. It then becomes an economic revolution and therefore a socialist revolution. The struggle for socialism has to be fought out by the masses, in every factory, by every proletarian against their employer. Only then will it become a socialist revolution.

Socialism will not and cannot be created by decrees; nor can it be established by any government, however socialist.

Socialism must be created by the masses—where the chains of capitalism are forged, there must they be broken.

Luxemburg argued the need was to "undermine the Scheidemann-Ebert government step by step", not to try and seize power before the conditions were ripe, but to fight "in every province, in every city, in every village, in every municipality, in order to transfer all the power of the state bit by bit from the bourgeoisie to the workers' and soldiers' councils".[205]

Her powerful, passionate speech won massive applause but the majority of the delegates did not grasp the key point she was making—that the decisive conflict for state power was still some considerable distance away and that what was needed now was revolutionary patience. The majority did vote for the following statement, which should have made Rosa's position absolutely clear:

The KPD will never take over governmental power except in response to the clear, unambiguous will of the great majority of the proletarian masses of all Germany, never except by the proletariat's conscious affirmation of the views, aims and methods of struggle of the KPD... The KPD will never enter the government just because Ebert and Scheidemann are going bankrupt and the USPD, by collaborating with them are in a blind alley.[206]

But the majority were far from patient, as the votes at conference proved. Events in the days ahead would pull the less cool-headed of the new KPD in the opposite direction and lead to catastrophe.

The conference had voted, against Luxemburg's advice, to boycott the forthcoming parliamentary elections. Luxemburg's position tallied with Lenin's. He argued that so long as workers have illusions in parliament and social democracy, revolutionaries have to participate in elections to break workers from their illusions. The difference was that Lenin won this position in his party. Even after the October Revolution the Bolsheviks had taken part in elections to the Constituent Assembly and had benefitted by doing so.

The KPD founding conference also voted to leave the official trade unions and call for "red" unions. Luxemburg knew such short-cuts, born out of frustration, would cut the KPD off from the mass of workers who were being radicalised. As Lenin responded in his pamphlet, *Left-Wing Communism: An Infantile Disorder*: "To refuse to work in the reactionary trade unions means leaving the insufficiently developed or backward masses of workers under the influence of the reactionary leaders".[207]

Berlin January 1919

Luxemburg's speech to the KPD launching conference on 30 December was an exhortation to revolutionary socialists in Germany to judge the situation realistically and focus on the hard graft of preparing for when social conditions would be ripe for the decisive struggle. She had written the new party's programme, arguing forcefully that the KPD could not take power without the support of the majority of the working class. Her approach was similar to Lenin's when in April 1917 he called for "all power to the soviets", but he went on to insist that for the time being the Bolsheviks could not impose their will but had to "patiently explain" the need to the rest of the working class.

Until early January the leaders of the new KPD thought the revolutionary wave would continue to mount but they did not expect an early or easy victory; they were certainly not planning to lead an uprising.

In the opening days of 1919 Berlin seemed like a city where nothing could stop the growth of the revolutionary left. Ebert's provisional government was hanging on to office and the USPD leaders abandoned it. The army was in chaos and the revolutionary left had real influence over the two most important army units in the city—the Marine Division and the Security Force, commanded by Berlin Police Chief Emil Eichhorn, a member of the USPD.

Ebert seriously considered abandoning Berlin to the revolutionaries and setting up a new government somewhere else to prepare for a counter-revolution. But the generals persuaded him to hold out and with their help the provisional government decided to provoke a military showdown in Berlin. Their opportunity came a few days later.

Ebert, Scheidemann, Noske and the other SPD leaders had determined to restore "law and order" and that meant decapitating the new KPD. Luxemburg and Liebknecht were the living embodiment of the movement that had toppled the Kaiser and ended the war. Ebert and the other SPD leaders needed to discredit them in the eyes of the masses; they did so by plotting with the military to provoke a rising in the city in January 1919, in order to crush it and blame the revolutionaries for any bloodshed.

> *The truth is: there was no Spartakus uprising.* Irrefutable proof of this is contained in the leading articles in *Rote Fahne* [the KPD newspaper], which faithfully mirrored the policy of the Spartakusbund during those critical days... The leaders of the KPD were reckoning on a steady development of the revolution and not in the least with an armed struggle on the streets of Berlin...
>
> The January fighting was cautiously and deliberately prepared and cunningly provoked by the leaders of the counter-revolution.[208]

On 4 January the right-wing Social Democrats made their move. Their provisional government sacked the popular Emil Eichhorn, the left-wing USPD member who had run the Berlin Police since the revolution. It was a deliberate provocation.

Empire and Revolution

The government knew that the Freikorps, the special mercenary force set up in collaboration with the generals to defeat the revolution, had built up enough forces outside Berlin to crush any coup from the left and retake the city by force, claiming it was restoring order. Sadly Liebknecht and some of the less experienced members of the newly-formed Communist Party walked right into this trap.

Many workers who had been prepared to tolerate Ebert's provisional government only weeks before now turned bitterly against it, protesting on 5 January against Eichhorn's sacking in what was described as "the biggest demonstration Berlin had ever known".

The response was far greater than anyone had expected.

> The workers, many of them armed, responded enthusiastically to militant speeches from Liebknecht, Daumig of the revolutionary shop stewards and from Ledebour of the USPD. The organisers had intended this to be a peaceful protest but the angry crowds were not willing to merely demonstrate and then go home.[209]

With very little encouragement the crowds rushed off to seize control of the newspapers—including the building of the SPD paper *Vorwärts*, an entire issue of which was dumped in the river. Later it was proved that this was led by paid, right-wing agents provocateur out to provoke an uprising.[210] Later, in a court trial held in Munich during 1925, General Groener admitted under oath Ebert's arrangements with his Army general staff: "As early as 29 December 1918, Ebert ordered Noske to lead troops against the Spartacists. The Freikorps assembled that day and everything was ready."

Noske took on the job of Defence Minister and was quite frank about his role: "Somebody must be the bloodhound".[211] On the day Eichhorn's dismissal was announced, Noske and Ebert were already secretly inspecting six Volunteer Corps of handpicked, right-wing officers on the outskirts of Berlin. Noske then met the leaders of the Volunteer Corps at Army Staff HQ, where the details of the march on the city were agreed.

The influential Berlin revolutionary shop stewards, who wavered between the USPD and the revolutionaries, now reacted to Eichhorn's sacking by calling for the overthrow of the provisional government. Luxemburg and the leadership of the Communist Party were opposed to this course of action. A few days earlier the KPD had distributed a leaflet arguing: "If the Berlin workers were today to disperse the national assembly and throw the Ebert-Scheidemann clique into prison, while the workers of the Ruhr, Upper Silesia and the rural workers of Germany east of the Elbe remained inactive, the capitalists would be able tomorrow to subdue Berlin through hunger". A meeting of the Communist Party's central committee on 4 January agreed unanimously: "It would be senseless...a government based on the Berlin proletariat would last two weeks and no longer".[212]

Yet only two days later Karl Liebknecht and Wilhelm Pieck, the party's representatives at a meeting of the revolutionary shop stewards, took it upon themselves to support a call for a general strike and a mass demonstration the next day to overthrow the government. Rosa Luxemburg was outraged when later she finally learned what they had done, but by then there was little that she and the rest of the leadership could do about it. Karl Radek of the Bolsheviks advised the party leadership to oppose the move openly and urge workers to stay within the limits of peaceful protest:

> The most advanced Berlin workers have been misled by the shop stewards, who lack any political experience and are not in a position to see the relationship of forces in the country as a whole. The shop stewards have impetuously turned the protest movement into a fight for power that will allow

Empire and Revolution

Scheidemann to deal the Berlin movement a blow that can set it back for months. The only restraining force that can prevent this is the Communist Party... I know this will lead to a decline in morale but that is nothing compared to what the masses will say to themselves after a bloodletting.[213]

Radek was absolutely right. There are occasions when revolutionaries have to restrain workers from cavalier adventurism and risk temporary unpopularity; this was certainly one of them. Rosa Luxemburg was against a rising because she knew it was unplanned and that the movement had not yet won the backing of the mass of workers. Yet she felt she could not follow Radek's advice.

Now the call had gone out for mass action on 6 January she feared the new Communist Party would lose the most militant workers if it told them on the very eve of a general strike to hold back from struggle; that they would think the new KPD was no different to the left Social Democrats of the USPD, who always vacillated between advance and retreat.

This was a big mistake. But on the day everything, at first, seemed to go well for the revolutionaries:

The General Strike was a massive success... Another massive demonstration paraded through the streets. Revolutionary workers seized all the bourgeois newspapers... The government printing offices had been taken over, as were the railway stations. Snipers on the Brandenburg Gate dominated the whole centre of the city. "Only a few strong points in the government quarter remained in government hands." At a meeting in the Chancellory Landsberg reported, "The Spartakists have taken over the Railway Administration Building. The Ministry of War is next, and then it is our turn".

But the revolution was not nearly as strong as it first seemed, nor the government as weak as it looked. Just as the workers seemed to be in control of inner Berlin, the

Revolutionary Committee began to hesitate and show its weakness—for it was not representative of the three bodies that constituted it. Liebknecht and Pieck had joined it for the KPD Spartacists but their leadership had not been consulted and strongly disapproved.

According to Radek it was not until a week later that Rosa Luxemburg learnt that Liebknecht had signed the call with Ledebour for the establishment of a "provisional government"... Liebknecht had allowed himself to be carried away with the idea of a Left Independent government and had kept this from the knowledge of the [Central Committee of the party].

The January fighting went down in history as the "Spartakist Uprising". But the Spartakist leadership of the Communist Party were opposed to the project! Such is the fate of revolutionaries who have the right policy, but who don't have a powerful disciplined party to put it into effect. They get the blame for actions they do not initiate and cannot control.

The revolutionary shop stewards were no more united behind the attempted seizure of power than the Spartakists. Their two most influential members in the Berlin factories—Richard Müller and Däumig—argued strongly against the action...

The USPD were, by their very nature, riven with internal divisions over this matter as over every other. They were soon to prove themselves the most dangerous and unreliable of allies in any bid for power.

The Revolutionary Committee was not only unrepresentative—it was also too large and unwieldy to direct any action, let alone a seizure of power. With 52 members it was a mini-parliament not an executive capable of co-ordinating the movements of revolutionary troops and armed workers. Instead of acting, it debated endlessly what to do.[214]

The effect on the morale of the workers and soldiers fighting in the streets was terrible. Paul Levi, one of the KPD leaders, wrote this eye witness account:

What was seen on Monday in Berlin was probably the greatest proletarian demonstration in history... From the City Hall to the Königsplatz the workers were standing shoulder to shoulder. They had bought along their weapons and their red flags. They were ready to do anything, to give everything, even their lives. There was an army of 200,000 such as Ludendorff had never seen. Then the inconceivable happened... The masses were standing from nine in the morning in the fog and cold. Somewhere their leaders were sitting and conferring. The fog lifted and the masses were still standing. Their leaders conferred. Noon came and in addition to the cold, hunger came. And the leaders conferred. The masses were feverish with excitement. They wanted one deed, one word but nobody knew what to do because the leaders were conferring.

The fog came again and with it the dusk. The masses went home sadly. They had wanted great things but they had done nothing because their leaders conferred. They sat the entire night and conferred. When dawn came they were still conferring.[215]

This "Revolutionary Committee", which had called for armed resistance and the overthrow of the government, proved utterly incapable of decisive leadership. According to Paul Frölich:

It issued an appeal for the demonstration and strike on 6 January, distributed some weapons to the forces in the imperial stables and made a feeble attempt to occupy the War Ministry. That was all. It did not bother about the armed workers who had occupied the newspaper offices; it assigned them no tasks and left them in buildings of no strategic importance whatsoever. The only measure of reasonable military value was taken by the workers themselves at their own initiative when the occupied the railway stations.[216]

Meanwhile the Revolutionary Committee spent days and nights in endless, fruitless discussion. It started clutching at straws by trying to open negotiations with the enemy—a move that only confused and demoralised the armed workers.

Counter-revolution, defeat and murder

As the revolutionary forces began to drift away, it soon became evident to all there was no hope of seizing power. On 10 January, with government troops pouring into the city and the counter-revolutionary Freikorps on the offensive, the KPD formally withdrew from the Revolutionary Committee, which had effectively collapsed, with the USPD and revolutionary shop stewards element of it attempting to negotiate a truce with the SPD.

However, at the same time thousands of armed workers were on the streets and the Spartacus leaders felt compelled to stay with them. Rosa Luxemburg regarded the negotiations between the Revolutionary Committee and the SPD as a trap. Again and again she appealed through the pages of *Rote Fahne* for deeds, not negotiations and she was right— but the damage had been done. The problem was that, unlike the Bolsheviks, the young KPD did not have the authority to take the leadership either in attack or in retreat.

On 13 January, by order of the SPD leaders, troops attacked the *Vorwärts* building occupied by the revolutionaries and murdered in cold blood the delegation sent to negotiate surrender. Mercenary head-hunters and Freikorps thugs were now scouring the city in search of the Spartacus leaders. The SPD paper *Vorwärts* had for weeks been encouraging the witch-hunt, calling openly for the murder of Luxemburg, Liebknecht and Radek.

Empire and Revolution

But Luxemburg and Liebknecht refused to leave Berlin, despite the SPD price on their heads. On the evening of 15 January, after being tipped off by a government spy inside the KPD, a unit of troops raided the house where Luxemburg, Liebknecht and Wilhelm Pieck were in hiding. They were taken to the headquarters of one of the Freikorps units operating under SPD approval, where they were "interrogated" and tortured.

That evening Liebknecht was "taken for questioning" and murdered in the Tiergarten. His killers drove the body to a first aid station and handed it over as that of "an unknown man". Rosa Luxemburg was clubbed with a soldier's rifle butt, shot in the head and thrown off a bridge into the Landwehr Canal, where her body washed up on 31 May 1919.

On 16 January *Vorwärts* was the first to announce the news. It did so trumpeting the lie that Liebknecht had been shot "while trying to escape" and that Luxemburg had been "killed by the people".

In December 1918 SPD minister Noske had agreed with the generals to set up the Freikorps as a special mercenary force. Drawn from the officers and the storm battalions of the Kaiser's army, it was reactionary and anti-Semitic. Its banners were often adorned with the swastika and many of its members were to become the cadre of the Nazi party. The Freikorps would be used again and again by the Social Democrats, most notably in the suppression of the Bavarian soviet in Munich. In the first half of 1919 the Freikorps marched through Germany attacking the very people who had made the November Revolution and voted Social Democrat in the January 1919 National Assembly election.

The German Revolution was far from over and there were many battles to come. In March 1919 there was renewed fighting in Berlin and it would be another five years before German capitalism could claim any real stability. But January was an important victory, which the ruling class could build on. In November their old state machine had been shattered and at the start of the January fighting the generals did not have enough troops at their command to control Berlin, let alone the whole German state. But the January debacle restored their monopoly of armed force and allowed them to increase the number of armed units they could depend upon.

The murder of Rosa Luxemburg, Karl Liebknecht and other leading revolutionaries such as Leo Jogiches was a great boost for the German ruling class. Luxemburg and Jogiches were experienced and had a good enough grasp of revolutionary politics to prevent further terrible mistakes. Rosa's murder in particular caused immense joy among the Berlin middle classes. Her successors were brave and talented but the revolution had lost its most able and experienced leader. The German working class would pay a terrible price for her loss. Her last article, "Order reigns in Berlin", published in *Rote Fahne* the day before she was murdered, blamed the defeat on "the contradiction between the powerful, resolute and offensive appearance of the Berlin masses on the one hand; and the irresoluteness, timidity and indecision of the Berlin leadership on the other".[217]

With a mass party, rooted and experienced like the Bolsheviks had become in the run-up to 1917, the German working class could have avoided Ebert's trap, or co-ordinated the revolutionary forces if an insurrection was started against its advice.

In April 1919 Trotsky wrote an article explaining why:

At the moment of its transition to open revolutionary struggle for political power, the German working class proved to be defenceless organisationally. The Russian working class, which accomplished its October Revolution, received a priceless legacy from the previous epoch: a centralised, revolutionary party. Fifty years of bitter struggles against

Tsarism prepared a large staff of revolutionary leaders, tempered in struggle and bound together by the unity of the revolutionary programme. History bequeathed nothing like this to the German working class. It was compelled not only to fight for power but to create its organisation and train future leaders in the very course of this struggle... Absent was a centralised revolutionary party with a combat leadership whose authority is universally accepted by the working masses.[218]

The November Revolution had toppled the Kaiser, finished off the old order and ended the First World War. The defeat of the January uprising and the murder of the KPD leadership was a terrible blow, but it was not the end of the German Revolution. On at least five occasions between 1918 and 1923 German capitalism was at serious risk.

Deliberate starvation

The uprising of the German people had brought the war to an end; they were thanked by the Allies with continued, deliberate starvation. The Allied naval blockade of Germany that was applied from the start of the war succeeded in restricting vital supplies and starved large numbers of the German population. It continued long after the armistice in November 1918 and had already contributed greatly to the reduction of the supplies of food to the Central Powers in the final year of the war. It spread death and disease, as famine encroached upon the civilian populations of Central Europe.

The prolongation of the blockade by the Allies for some eight months after the ceasefire was portrayed as a strategy to prevent the resurgence of German military power, but it was deliberately used to suppress revolutionary upheavals in Germany and in the states of the former Austro-Hungarian Empire.

The post-armistice food blockade against Germany was applied with particular severity until the end of March 1919 and was then partially raised until 12 July 1919 when it was ended by the Treaty of Versailles. In the months of October and November 1918, famine conditions were prevalent in many cities and industrial regions. From 1914 the blockade had contributed gradually to a reduction of 50 percent in the supply of food to the population.

From the end of the shooting war to the conclusion of the state of hostilities, the continued food blockade brought about a quarter of a million additional deaths among the civilian population of Germany.[219]

13

Revolution in Europe and beyond

"The whole of Europe is filled with the spirit of revolution. There is a deep sense not only of discontent but of anger and revolt amongst the workers... The whole existing order in its political, economic and social aspects, is questioned by the mass of the population from one end of Europe to the other"
—*David Lloyd George, March 1919*[220]

The revolutionary wave swept across all the defeated nations, burying along with the Russian Tsar and the German Kaiser Turkey's Ottoman Empire and Austro-Hungary's Hapsburg Empire.

The pressure was too much for the rickety, multi-national monarchy, heir to the Holy Roman Empire born 1,200 years before. Its army collapsed and the middle class leaders of the national minorities seized control of the major cities. Czechs and Slovaks took over Prague, Brno and Bratislava; supporters of a unified "Yugoslav" state took over Zagreb and Sarajevo; Hungarians under the liberal aristocrat Michael Karoly held Budapest; and the Poles took Cracow.

Huge crowds stormed through Vienna demanding a republic and tearing down imperial emblems, but power in the German speaking part of Austria passed into the hands of a Social Democrat-led coalition with the bourgeois parties. Czechoslovakia and Bulgaria contained large numbers of revolutionary workers opposed to the middle class nationalism of their new governments. Revolutionaries led the unemployed in an attempt to storm the Austrian parliament.[221]

The US Ambassador in Paris expressed the same fears that Lloyd George had communicated to Clemenceau in March 1919: "Bolshevism is gaining ground everywhere".[222] His immediate concern was that workers had just taken power in Hungary, replacing the liberal-nationalist regime established at the end of 1918.

Even the victor states, Italy, France and Britain, were rocked by mass strikes and social upheavals of varying intensity. Revolt also spread to neutral countries like Holland, Sweden and Spain, where a new wave of militancy erupted in 1918. In southern Spain the years 1918-20 were known as the "Three Bolshevik Years" (*Trienio Bolchevista*) and there were mass strikes in Barcelona and throughout Catalonia. There were riots in Paris, Lyon and Copenhagen.

The rising tide of struggle was not restricted to Europe. There was a massive dock strike in Bombay and 1919 saw mass strikes throughout Australia, Canada, the US and Brazil.

Britain on the brink of revolution
At the end of the war Britain faced a war for Irish independence and colonial revolts in India, China, Egypt, Mesopotamia and in the Caribbean, where discontent among de-mobbed West Indian soldiers fused with the anger of workers protesting against the economic hardships caused by the war.

Between 1916 and 1919 British West Indian colonies including St Lucia, Grenada, Barbados, Antigua, Trinidad, Jamaica and British Guiana experienced a wave of violent strikes. And it was into this turmoil that the disgruntled troops of the British West Indies Regiments arrived after mutinying against racism while on service in Italy at the end of the war. The British government sent battleships to the Caribbean as disenchanted workers and demobilised soldiers rioted in Jamaica, Grenada and British Honduras. A secret memo admitted, "Nothing we can do will alter the fact that the black man has begun to think and feel as good as the white".[223]

General Sir Henry Wilson, Chief of the Imperial General Staff, wrote that he feared "the loss of Ireland to begin with; the loss of Empire in the second place and the loss of England itself to finish with. I have not been so nervous about the state of affairs in regard to the British Empire since July 1914 and in many ways I am more anxious today than I was even that fateful month".[224]

Cabinet papers of the time reveal a British ruling class terrified that Britain itself was on the brink revolution. The police had gone on strike and the threat of a British general strike and serious mutinies in the armed forces convinced the Lloyd George government to abandon plans to send British troops to help reactionary forces overthrow the Bolshevik government.

In 1919 the industrial and political class struggle in Britain rose to unprecedented heights. Sir Henry Wilson told the cabinet that in his view "a Bolshevik rising was likely".[225] The head of Special Branch, Basil Thomson, warned that "February 1919 was the high watermark of revolutionary danger".[226]

Disaffection was rampant throughout the armed forces. In January 20,000 soldiers mutinied in Calais demanding repatriation. Another 10,000 soldiers mutinied at Folkestone and refused to return to France while a further 4,000 demonstrated in solidarity at Dover. In the same week 1,500 soldiers at Osterley Park demonstrated outside the war office. There was a mutiny on board HMS Kilbride, when sailors hauled the red flag up the masthead declaring: "Half the navy are on strike and the other half soon will be".[227] In May there were big police strikes in London and Liverpool. The state could not rely on its "armed bodies of men" during the crisis of 1919.

But the question of working class leadership returned to haunt the British movement. When the revolution erupted in Russia the Bolsheviks had 20,000 members and a cadre that had been schooled through 14 years of independent, revolutionary activity under illegal conditions. It had a thriving press that was read and sold by the best worker militants. In Britain there was no party, or even the beginnings of a party, like the Bolsheviks. Had one existed it could have grown massively during 1919.

The year began with a bang. The Clyde Workers' Committee (CWC) held a conference of shop stewards in shipbuilding and engineering on 5 January 1919 to launch a strike for a 40 hour week. It aimed to force the employers to absorb the rising unemployment created by demobilisation and the end of the munitions boom by limiting the hours of existing workers.

John Maclean made desperate appeals for the engineers to link up with the miners, who were themselves about to launch a national struggle. In 1919 the miners were demanding a 30 percent wage increase, a reduction in the working week and nationalisation of the pits. Because of the urgent need for coal they were in a powerful position. The issue of nationalisation was being forced upon the coal owners and the government by the threat of mass action from below; it would be a highly political strike and a big threat to the ruling class.

Maclean understood what was at stake. Throughout January he had been campaigning for the Miners' Reform Movement in the Scottish and South Wales coalfields. In January the Miners' Federation Conference was held in Southport. Maclean spent a week in the Lancashire coalfield organising unofficial committees in preparation for what he hoped would be a national coal strike.

He was not present at the start of the 40 hours strike in Glasgow. But he urged the engineers to wait until the miners struck and throw their weight behind an all-out challenge to the ruling class. The CWC ignored Maclean, and did not bother to contact the rest of the National Shop Stewards' Movement. Although Maclean believed the 40 hours strike was premature, once it was in motion he campaigned hard for its victory:

> The strike on the Clyde has been precipitated by general discontent expressed at hosts of workshop and union meetings and by the anxiety of the union officials not to let the matter slip out of their hands, lest they be supplanted by industrial unionism. Into the conflict then, let this be the class war started at last.[228]

MacLean's comments about the anxiety of the union officials hit the mark. The 40 hours strike was controlled by the Scottish TUC and the executive of the Glasgow Trades Council, and although the CWC was included on the organising committee it was hamstrung by officialdom. The strike committee chairman was Manny Shinwell, a trade union official and a member of the ILP. Before the strike began he publicly stressed the reformist aims of the officials: "This movement is NOT revolutionary in character. It is attributable solely and entirely to the fear of possible unemployment".[229]

The strike ranks as a key moment in the development of the revolutionary movement in Britain. The abiding symbol of Red Clydeside is the raising of the red flag in Glasgow's George Square during the strike. But Lloyd George and Winston Churchill had prepared for the worst. Under secret cabinet orders 10,000 troops had been placed on standby for imminent dispatch to Clydeside if required.

The strike began at the end of January and the Clyde valley ground to a halt. 40,000 struck on the first day and the numbers swelled.

The government knew that a workers' victory would

mean disaster for the ruling class. But the union officials were more in control than had been the case during wartime and their aims were far from revolutionary. Yet Churchill, Minister of Labour, urged caution. The army command explained that a massive show of force was risky with the army unreliable. Churchill concluded the best strategy was "a judicious use of force at an opportune moment" combined with support from the union leaders. [230]

After a week there was a virtual general strike on Clydeside with over 100,000 out indefinitely. Mass flying pickets of thousands had gone from factory to factory and closed everything in their path. The key feature of the picketing was that it involved large numbers of women, young people and unemployed soldiers. Lloyd George had promised the troops they would return to a "Land fit for heroes"—instead they faced the prospect of mass unemployment. One returning soldier told how "More than anything I hated to see war-crippled men standing in the gutter selling matches. We had been promised a land fit for heroes; it took a hero to live in it. I'd never fight for my country again". [231]

The 40 hours strike saw the start of organisation among the unemployed. The war had brought a dramatic increase in the numbers of women at work and at its end women were usually the first to be sacked. By January 1919 there were thousands of unemployed women workers in Glasgow. The Scottish section of the Federation of Women Workers fully supported the strike. In Clydebank a special meeting of women workers in the town voted to join the strike and they did so actively, picketing out all the apprentices. Similar support came from women in Bridgeton, Partick, Govan and Dumbarton. The *Paisley Express* reported the energy with which women textile workers picketed: "It was noted that the women were not silent onlookers but showed more zeal and demonstrated more in speech than the men". [232]

The strike had spread to the shipyards at Greenock and Port Glasgow. On the Forth, the naval dockyards at Rosyth, Leith shipyards and over 1,000 workers at Grangemouth were on strike. So too were large numbers of printers and engineers in Edinburgh. 36,000 miners had come out on unofficial sympathy strike in the Lanarkshire and Fife coalfields, as had 10,000 iron moulders. Despite the lack of effort by the leaders to spread the action, Belfast and Barrow were paralysed too. The strike was even more solid in Belfast, where the city was paralysed by a virtual general strike.

The key moment was Bloody Friday—31 January 1919. That morning 35,000 strikers and unemployed soldiers marched into Glasgow's George Square demanding a reduction in hours. Government figures indicate that apart from the 35,000 on the march, there were another 25,000 supporters gathered around the square. Reporters from the major British and European newspapers—including the young war poet Siegfried Sassoon—were waiting to witness the events. The authorities deliberately provoked the confrontation that followed.

The police baton-charged the demonstration but the crowds fought back driving off the police. The strikers then marched to a rally in Glasgow Green. Willie Gallacher, Chairman of the CWC, was bludgeoned over the head by police and then arrested for incitement to riot. This provocation, planned by the cabinet, was the "opportune moment" Churchill had been waiting for.

The strike leaders were seized and that evening the troops held on standby flooded into the city.

Next morning Glasgow was like an armed camp. Throughout the night trainloads of young English soldiers had been brought to the city—young lads of 19 or so who had no idea of where they were or why they were there. The authorities did not dare use the local regiments at Maryhill barracks, in case they supported the strikers. The whole city bristled with tanks and machine guns.[233]

The *Glasgow Herald* reported: "The panic of the civic and national authorities can only be explained thus—they actually believed a Spartacus uprising was planned to start in the city and they were prepared to suppress it at all costs".[234]

Electricians threatened to black out London and engineers in Sheffield, Manchester, London and Tyneside were on the verge of walking out. But once the army had been mobilised by the cabinet, attacks on the strike by the press and the union officials were orchestrated. The strike committees in Glasgow, London and Belfast—the three most militant areas—were suspended by their own union leaders and strike pay suspended too. The mass picketing was called off on the understanding an official national strike would be called. But this was a ruse by the union leaders.

The strike petered out with Glasgow transformed into an armed camp. But according to Maclean the strike was defeated "more by lack of working class ripeness, than batons, tanks and machine guns". The mass picketing and giant demonstrations had shown the potential power of the working class—but without clear-sighted revolutionary leadership from its own ranks that potential was blocked by the trade union leaders.

In his book *Revolt on the Clyde* Willie Gallacher argues: "We were leading a strike when we should have been leading a revolution. A rising was expected—a rising should have taken place".[235]

He was wrong; they were not leading a revolution at that point. But if the leadership had led the strike as revolutionaries they could have won an important victory. Instead they acted as if the Clyde existed in isolation, ignoring the links with the shop stewards' organisations in Sheffield, London,

Barrow, Belfast and all the mining centres across Britain.

If the strike leaders had maintained the mass picketing instead of calling it off when the army appeared; if they'd marched the 35,000 from George Square to Maryhill Barracks instead of Glasgow Green; and if delegations had gone to the coalfields and into England, they could have beaten a terrified ruling class.

After all, 1919 was the year of European revolutions and the year when the Irish War of Independence exploded. Victory for the 40 hours strike would have terrified an already worried British ruling class and opened up the road to revolution. Whatever the shortcomings of their leaders, the strikers on the Clyde were not parochial in outlook. In reporting the Bombay dockworkers' strike, the *Strike Bulletin* proudly proclaimed: "A victory in Scotland will help our comrades in India, who are with us heart and soul".[236]

Lloyd George, the miners and the union leaders

In 1919 there were over a million miners in Britain, organised in the Miners' Federation. In pithead ballots they had voted massively for an all-out strike in support of a 30 percent wage rise, a two hour reduction in the working day and nationalisation. Maclean believed the miners struggle was key because it had the potential to unite the whole working class in a confrontation with capital.

Wartime super profits meant the coal owners could afford concessions on wages and conditions—but nationalisation on the miners' terms was a different matter. It was a political threat to the employing class, who wanted an end to the state control that had been essential during wartime. With the war over and unemployment set to rise, the miners' struggle was a defining moment. The government was not in a strong position. It played for time and proposed the setting up of a Royal Commission to look into the miners' demands. In his autobiography Nye Bevan tells how the miners' leader

Robert Smillie described the meeting between Lloyd George and the Union leaders:

Lloyd George sent for the leaders and they went, determined not to be talked over by the eloquent Welshman. "He was quite frank with us from the outset" said Smillie. "He said to us, 'Gentlemen, you have fashioned, in the Triple Alliance of the unions represented by you, a most powerful instrument. I feel bound to tell you that we are at your mercy. The army is disaffected and cannot be relied upon. Trouble has already occurred in a number of camps. We have just emerged from a great war and the people are eager for the reward of their sacrifices but we are in no position to satisfy them. If you carry out your threat you will defeat us. But if you do', asked Lloyd George, 'have you weighed the consequences? The strike will be in defiance of the Government of the country and by its very success, will precipitate a constitutional crisis of the first importance. For if a force arises in the state which is stronger than the state itself, then it must be ready to take on the functions of the state or withdraw and accept the authority of the state. Gentlemen', asked the Prime Minister quietly, 'have you considered, and if you have, are you ready?' From that moment", said Smillie, "We were beaten and we knew it".[237]

The union leaders were terrified of the consequences and settled for accepting the Sankey Coal Commission, which they tried to sell to the miners as a victory. The government's compromise was a trap to disarm the miners and avoid a confrontation it could not win. But their strategy worked—thanks to the union leaders, who sold the compromise to the rank and file.

The Sankey Commission was a turning point in British working class history. By accepting it, the trade union leaders spurned the best opportunity to challenge the capitalist class and snatched defeat from the jaws of victory. Lloyd George and his cabinet recognised the conservative role played by the Labour and trade union leaders. He knew in periods of acute crisis they would stick with the status quo rather than risk revolution. As the Tory leader Bonar Law said, "Trade union organisation was the only thing between us and anarchy—without it our position was hopeless".[238]

A national railway strike was the next major crisis for the government. The railway workers were the most powerful group of all but their leader, Jimmy Thomas, was the archetypal right winger. Try as he might, he could not stop a national strike breaking out in September 1919. But he did manage to end it within nine days. The rail strike was followed by a strike of 65,000 foundry workers and a series of other disputes across the country. But each struggle was isolated and the opportunity for all-out confrontation with a worried ruling class had been thrown away.

Had the Communist Party been formed in 1918 or early 1919 it could have taken advantage of a great opportunity. Unfortunately it wasn't formed until the end of 1920, when the tide had turned in favour of the employers. The post-war boom collapsed into slump and rising unemployment sapped working class confidence. And because the trade union leaders had rescued the ruling class in 1919, the employers were able to launch an offensive and break the back of the powerful shop stewards' movement.

As the labour historian James Hinton has argued:

there is good reason to re-examine the last great revolutionary period in British history... The history of the British labour movement between 1910 and the early 1920s has a special claim to our attention...these years mark a climax of class-conscious self-activity among the workers which, in Britain, has not yet been surpassed...

Whatever distortions were later to be imposed on the British revolutionary movement by its subordination to the heirs of a degenerated Russian Revolution, the post-war victory of the theory of soviet power over both syndicalism and parliamentarianism rested upon the authentic, if ambiguous, experience of a section of the British working class movement during the war years. It is an experience that deserves to be rescued from oblivion.[239]

Italy's two red years

In the last year of the war Italian industry developed rapidly and the working class grew enormously. Victory on the battlefront did not bring the Italian ruling class any territory or spoils of war. Nor did it bring social peace. Italy was torn apart in the *biennio rosso*, the "two red years". War-weary workers started a wave of strikes and flocked into the unions and the Socialist Party.

The summer of 1919 saw a three-day general strike in solidarity with the Russian Revolution. In the spring of 1920 Turin workers fought a bitter and unsuccessful strike to make the employers recognise the factory councils—championed by the Marxist Antonio Gramsci as embryonic soviets.

In August engineering workers in Milan reacted to an employers' lockout by occupying the factories. Within four days the movement had spread throughout the country. Over half a million workers occupied the factories, set up councils to run them and reached out for political power. They began to make and store weapons in the factories. Armed workers' guards defended the occupied factories and the workers kept production going because they believed they were making a new society based on workers' control.

Gramsci was key to the Turin factory council movement that grouped around his newspaper, *L'Ordine Nuovo* (New Order). The councils organised all workers, regardless of union. Gramsci connected the example of working class power which had emerged in Russia with the experience of workers in other countries:

We say the present period is revolutionary precisely because we can see that the working class in all countries is tending to generate from within itself, proletarian institutions of a new type, representative in basis and industrial in arena. We say the present period is revolutionary because the working class tends with all its energy and all its power to found its own state.[240]

The government was paralysed and the Italian state seemed on the point of collapse. In the south the peasants returning from the war had begun to take over and divide the land. Prime Minister Giolitti would not move against the workers for fear of unleashing a civil war he couldn't win. Instead he wagered that the trade union leaders would concede a peaceful outcome to the dispute and that the Socialist Party leaders would go along with it, leaving the bosses free to fight another day.

That is precisely what happened. The Socialist Party decided the occupations were the responsibility of the union leaders and a special union congress decided by a majority of three to two to reject calls for revolution and reach a negotiated settlement with the bosses. The rank and file felt demoralised and defeated. They had fought for revolution yet all they got were improvements in pay and conditions.

"It is our glory and our pride that we prevented the outbreak of revolution, which the extremists desired", boasted D'Aragona, the secretary of FIOM, the metal workers' trade union.[241] In 1922 the ruling class backed and financed Mussolini's fascists and he got rid of trade union and Socialist Party leaders as well as "extremists" like Gramsci.

For a month the workers had taken over the factories and run them. It was an incredible achievement. The occupations were spreading until the union leaders brought the movement to a halt. If the factory council movement could have broken out beyond Turin then the outcome could have been different. But the militants who wanted to extend the struggle and carry it towards an insurrection had no contact with each other and no contact with the peasants, ex-soldiers and landless labourers fighting in the south. By the time Gramsci had grasped the need to break with the reformist leadership of the Socialist Party and launch the new Italian Communist Party, the occupations were over.

Gramsci spent the last ten years of his life in a fascist prison. Looking back in 1924 wrote:

> During 1919-20 we committed very serious errors, which we are now paying for in full. For fear of being called careerists, we did not form a separate fraction and try to organise it throughout Italy. We did not make the Turin factory councils into an independent directing centre, which could have exercised an immense influence over the whole country, for fear of splitting the trade unions and of being prematurely expelled from the Socialist Party.[242]

Postscript for the reformists

The reformist leaders of the German SPD and the Italian Socialist Party, who rejected revolution and helped defeat it, did so believing that once the threat of revolution was removed life would return to normal. They assumed that things would continue just as they were before the war with the peaceful expansion of capitalism and the spread of democracy. History has shown just how wrong they were.

During the occupation of the factories in 1920, Benito Mussolini was a nationally known figure in Italy. He was a bombastic rabble-rouser and the former editor of the Socialist Party newspaper *Avanti*, but he had broken with his party in 1914 to support the war and Italian national-ism. His political following was small, restricted to a group of confused ex-socialists who, like him, had become chau-vinists. In addition he had a following among a few frontline soldiers who believed Italy, as a victor nation, had been denied its right to territory in Austria and the Adriatic coast.

In March 1919 Mussolini formed the first *fascio de combattimento* (fascist fighting unit). They did badly in the Italian election that year and were sidelined as the factory occupations exploded to challenge the bosses and the state.

The ending of the occupations and the subsequent demoralisation boosted Mussolini's fortunes and the Italian bosses turned to him to smash the working class. The Socialist Party leaders were jailed and persecuted when Mussolini came to power. His success won admiration from ruling classes elsewhere in Europe—Winston Churchill was full of praise for Mussolini's methods in dealing with the left.

In Germany the SPD made every effort to turn a developing working class revolution back into the more acceptable form of a bourgeois democracy. To do so it created the armed gangs of ex-officers in the Freikorps. It then unleashed them to murder workers throughout 1919 and smash up the developing workers' councils.

The right-wing leadership of the SPD bears responsibility for the murder of many of the best leaders of the German working class. But in 1920 the Freikorps thugs moved from attacking the left to attacking those same reformist leaders. Later the Freikorps elements provided the basis for Hitler's Nazis when they attacked and persecuted the trade unions and the SPD as well as the communists.

14

The war after the war

"Do not cry, do not laugh, but understand"
—*Spinoza*

The First World War was a clash of empires in which the various ruling classes were prepared for any number of dead to advance their imperial interests. Yet the war provoked a revolutionary wave, which brought it to an end.

While the Bolshevik Revolution enabled the German High Command to concentrate its manpower and resources on the Western Front in early 1918, the irony is that the triumph of the Russian working class gave inspiration and impetus to the workers' and soldiers' movement throughout Germany, which brought the war to an abrupt end in November 1918.

The Russian Revolution brought hope to the German workers because it was a revolt against the hated First World War and its millions of dead. But it was also a blow against the system that produced the war. The revolution raised the horizons of the reluctant German conscripts in the trenches, the ordinary sailors of the Imperial Navy and the suffering masses on the home front. It fired their combined struggle to such an extent that they toppled the Kaiser, forced an armistice on the warmongers and brought a swift end to four and a half years of barbarism.

But, as we have seen, the social democratic leaders sold out the struggles that swept across Europe between 1917 and 1920. In Germany, Austria and Italy the workers' movements were destroyed, leaving the new Russian republic isolated and under attack. Under such conditions the workers' democracy in Russia could not survive for too long. As Rosa Luxemburg had warned in early 1918: "Everything that happens in Russia is comprehensible and represents an inevitable chain of causes and effects, the starting point and the real end term of which are; the failure of the German proletariat and the occupation of Russia by German imperialism".[243]

To the victors, the spoils

Under the Treaty of Versailles Germany was forced to hand over a quarter of all its coal supplies as reparation to France, Belgium and Italy. The Allies also demanded the secession of large chunks of German territory, the handover of all her overseas colonies, the payment of huge sums of money in reparations and a signed statement recognising Germany's "war guilt".

The German military was reduced and it had to hand over large amounts of weaponry. The French took possession of the Rhine Bridgeheads. The left bank of the Rhine was demilitarised and the right neutralised. Once in Germany, the Allied army of occupation would have the right to requisition anything it needed. The Germany navy had to surrender most of its warships and it was not allowed an air force. The war devastated the German economy. The Allied blockade had cut the country off from the world market. Run as a war economy for four years, it was kept going only by cutting workers' living standards below subsistence level.

When the war ended Germany's markets had been taken over by the victorious powers and industrial production in 1920 was half its pre-war level.

The Versailles Treaty laid the basis for a greater barbarism 20 years later. Lloyd George, key architect of Versailles, admitted as much at the time: "We shall have to fight another war all over again in 25 years".[244]

For German workers wartime living standards continued

long after the war. Over 700,000 Germans had died of starvation and malnutrition between 1914 and 1918. In the months of October and November 1918, famine conditions were prevalent in many cities and industrial regions.

The ordinary German civilians who suffered so much during the war were not exempted from the humiliation of defeat. For them the most direct consequence was the continuation of the food blockade until the Versailles Treaty was signed in July 1919. Part of the reason for continuing the food blockade was to demoralise the German population and discourage "Bolshevism". It probably had the opposite effect. "The Winter of 1918-1919, even more than the war years, determined the Germans' and Austrians' folk memories of hunger as an instrument of war".[245]

Extending the British Empire

Britain and France in particular used the victory to grab the spoils of war at the Versailles peace settlement in 1919.

> Britain proceeded to divide up the Middle East with the French, took its pick of Germany's colonies and even cast its acquisitive eyes over parts of the Russian Empire, a former ally that collapsed in revolution in 1917. There were those in the Lloyd George government, including foreign secretary, Lord Curzon, who advocated the establishment of British protectorates over the Caucasus and Transcaspia".[246]

The imperial victors parcelled out the world between themselves and to suit themselves, and they set up a League of Nations to cover their tracks. Lenin described it as "a thieves' kitchen". Another 1.8 million square miles and 13 million people were added to the British Empire, including Palestine, Jordan and Iraq.

The war brought a fresh British Empire in the Middle East. This development was triggered by the war with Turkey. The British government regularised its occupation

Empire and Revolution

in Egypt, not by annexation or by making Egypt self-governing, but by declaring a protectorate and thereby seizing the titular over-lordship from Turkey, allowing the British to tighten their effective control over the country.

They constructed a great new strategic base at Suez, unprecedented in sheer magnitude—a bottomless sinkhole for imperial resources and manpower. A Suez "fixation" came into being that was to affect Britain's imperial consciousness in the years ahead. The Sykes-Picot Agreement of 1916 carved up the Levant on Anglo French lines; the more dismal the stalemate in France, the more alluring this Eastern promise became.

The idea circulated that what might be eventually lost in Alsace, Poland or Serbia, could be recouped, to the British benefit at least, in the Middle East. In this respect Lloyd George's elevation to Prime Minister was a crucial watershed.

Having gained power on the basis of winning the war at all costs, he set out to configure the conflict in ways that were capable of yielding to Britain the prizes that might make peace acceptable.[247]

It was Lloyd George's attempt to switch the balance of British aggression from the Germans to the Turks that underlay his bitter rivalry with the Army High Command. In April 1917 the British cabinet ordered an offensive into Palestine. The instructions were to capture Jerusalem by Christmas.

When the Turks abandoned the Holy City on 9 December [1917], the bells of Westminster Abbey were rung out for the first time since the war began. This was, for Britain, the climax of the conflict on the Eastern world. After the capture of Jerusalem, Lloyd George's Eastern vision was to ensure that Britain "shall be there by right of conquest, and shall remain".

It was in the final phase of the war that Lloyd George bought off the French with Lebanese and Syrian spheres of influence and at the same time aligned Britain with Zionism—encouraged by the Balfour Declaration on a Jewish "Homeland" in Palestine, issued on 2 November 1917. The supremacy of the British armies throughout the world of Islam was perhaps the most astonishing consequence of the war. Certainly it was the one that stored up most troubles and embarrassments for the future.

If in the disintegrating Ottoman world, Lloyd George had found the kind of war the British wanted to fight in the first place, the parallel events in France were more sombre.[248]

In 1919 British imperial supremacy seemed assured. But the celebrations were short lived as the Empire was rocked by revolts in Ireland, Egypt, Mesopotamia, India, China and the West Indies—and all at a time when the government was worried about a revolution in Britain, with mass strikes, mutinies in the army and navy, and strikes in the police.

Bombing Iraq, 1920

The origin of Iraq shows just how fundamentally imperialism has shaped the Middle East. At the end of the war, Britain was given a mandate by the League of Nations to oversee former Mesopotamia—redrawn on the map and called Iraq following the collapse of the Ottoman Empire in 1918. Ostensibly Britain had a peacekeeping role in the new Iraq, to prevent tribal feuds and improve the lot of the people.

But the real reason was to safeguard British investments, protect vital oil supplies and establish a useful staging post en route to India and the Far East. Britain created the Kingdom of Iraq but ran the country through an Indian-style administration, backed by a powerful military presence.

Throughout the 1920s Britain justified meddling in Middle East affairs by claiming it was liberating the people from the tyranny of the Turkish Empire, just as Bush and Blair claimed to be liberating Iraq from the tyranny of Saddam Hussein in 2003. It was soon clear the British had no intention of leaving and they faced rebellion in 1920. The RAF responded with air strikes, claiming they could hit rebels with surgical precision. The indiscriminate bombing of towns, villages, people and their cattle suggested otherwise.

An old socialist joke, originating in the Fife mining community at the end of the First World War, hit the nail on the head: "The sun never sets on the British Empire. Why? God couldn't trust the imperialists in the dark".[249]

Then and now

Ever since 1914, war has become as normal a capitalist mechanism as boom and slump. The 20th century spawned enough bloody wars to have depopulated our entire planet in previous eras. Rosa Luxemburg, in opposing the First World War, warned that humanity faced a stark choice: "Either the continuation of capitalism, new wars and a very early decline into chaos and anarchy, or the abolition of capitalist exploitation."

Then, competition between manufactured products gave rise to competition between especially nasty products called Dreadnoughts, machine guns and poison gas. In today's arms race competition is between weapons of mass destruction, to which the armoury of 1914 bears no comparison—nuclear warheads and submarines, neutron bombs, cluster bombs and stealth bombers.

Since 1914 the world has seen ever greater barbarism—the Second World War, the Holocaust and Hiroshima. Capitalism's capacity for barbarism is far greater now than it was in 1914 or even 1945. It is a system that starves millions to death and threatens to disfigure the planet and destroy humanity, either through ecological catastrophe, nuclear war, or both.

The prelude to the First World War was imperial rivalry in south east Europe, where war by proxy was fought out in 1912 and 1913.

Already this century, the same imperial rivalry has been played out in Georgia, South East Asia, Central Africa and most notably the Middle East. The latest instalment in the Ukraine and Crimea involves the big capitalist blocs. Not all local or regional conflicts lead to war but many do.

The war after the war

At the end of the Cold War we were promised that globalisation would bring peace and prosperity. But similar arguments were made in the run up to 1914. Karl Kautsky and other leading thinkers claimed that as capitalism developed it reduced the tendency to war. Lenin and Bukharin argued that the drive to war would continue so long as capitalism survived. John Maclean agreed. In 1917, inspired by the October Revolution, he produced his pamphlet, *The War after the War*, to convince workers of the need for revolution:

> The increased output of commodities will necessitate larger markets and hence a larger empire. The same applies to other capitalist countries. This must develop a more intense economic war than led to the present war and so precipitate the world into a bloodier business than we are steeped in now. We see preparations for this war after the war by the government, which works hand in hand with the growing industrial trusts for the monopoly of markets outside the Empire. Every other capitalist country is doing the same, especially in the US, which is getting a foothold in South and Central America and is manoeuvring with Japan for a firmer grip over the economic life of China.
>
> To avoid a recurrence of the present world crash on a bigger scale than before, the dumping of each nation's surplus

on "undeveloped" countries must be avoided by eliminating this surplus. Since this is due to workers having to sell their labour power as a commodity to the owners of land and capital, it is necessary that the need to sell labour power to any one must be abolished. This can only be accomplished by the ending of the class ownership of land and capital, by people taking possession of the whole means of living and using them co-operatively for creative purposes. Under such circumstances alone will it be possible for classes and class warfare to be abolished and for national antagonism and world wars to be stamped out forever. The Bolsheviks in Russia have given the world the lead.[250]

The First World War brought the world working class closer to its own emancipation than at any other time in history. It triggered a massive European social crisis that lasted into the 1920s and inspired colonial rebellion across the globe. At the end of 1917 the working class was in power in a major country for the first time, and for a brief few years a socialist world was a distinct possibility.

Another world war

The Second World War provided horrific confirmation of Lenin and Bukharin's theory of imperialism. In opposition to Kautsky, they had insisted the great powers would be forced to move from peace to war as they strove to partition and repartition the world. This is exactly what happened in the 1930s, in response to an unprecedented world slump and a recurrence, on a more intense basis, of the tensions that culminated in the First World War.

The established colonial powers, notably Britain and France, were able to rely upon their existing empires, enlarged by the seizure of former German colonies and much of the Middle East. The US was also able to increase its influence, particularly in Latin America. Chris Harman explains:

The world's second industrial power, Germany, was restricted to an even narrower national territory than in 1914. It had lost its colonies and France had made a series of alliances in Eastern Europe directed at reducing German influence there—even over German speaking Austria. In the Far East expanding Japanese capitalism felt similarly penned in by the colonial rule exercised by the French, the British, the Dutch and the US—as well as by the continuing British and French concessions in China...

Once the path of military expansion had been decided it fed upon itself. Every successful imperial adventure increased this—the Japanese takeover of Manchuria, the German annexation of Austria and then Czechoslovakia. But at the same time it increased the hostility of the existing empires—leading to the need for a greater arms production and further military adventures. The breaking points were the German seizure of western Poland and the Japanese onslaught on Pearl Harbour.

Once the logic of German expansion forced it to move on from its victories over Poland, Belgium and France and to push into the Ukraine, Russia was forced into the war in 1941. A few months later the US was too, as the logic of Japanese imperialism led it to try and grab the poorly defended Far East possessions of all the Western capitalisms.[251]

The Second World War is sometimes portrayed as a "good war". Many of those who fought believed they were fighting fascism and for a better world than the one they'd struggled through in the 1930s. But the war between the Axis and Allied power blocks was generated and driven by imperialist rivalry and was fought for imperialist interests. All but a handful of countries were involved. Many of the major cities were destroyed or severely damaged—Berlin and most German cities, Warsaw, Stalingrad, St Petersburg,

Rotterdam, Hiroshima, Nagasaki, London, Coventry and many more. Fifty million died, including 28 million civilians.

A world to win

Much has changed since Lenin and Bukharin developed their pioneering work to explain the outbreak of the First World War. Since national liberation movements kicked out the colonialists in the post-war period, imperialism has generally managed to exploit what are referred to as "developing" countries and dictate to weaker states quite effectively without direct colonial rule.

Today capitalism is more multinational than it has ever been but that doesn't mean relations between the great powers have become more harmonious. On the contrary competition and conflict are more intense. On the essential point Lenin is vindicated: capitalism leads to war. The evidence is there every day in the news.

War is an inevitable and recurring feature of the system we all live under—a world system whose driving force is the compulsion to accumulate profit. It is the bloodiest, most belligerent form of society in human history and as it grows older, its capacity for barbarism only increases.

The purpose of this book is to present the socialist case against the First World War and to commemorate those who opposed it—not just because they were right to do so but because we will have to learn from them. If we are to end war a new generation will have to take inspiration from their endeavours and learn from their victories and their defeats. After all we have a world to win.

NOTES

1   Robert Fisk, preface, *The Great War for Civilisation* (London, 2005).

2   Figures from Adam Hochschild, quoted in *Socialist Worker*, 1 February 2014.

3   Engels's 1887 preface to a pamphlet by Sigismund Borkheim, *In Memory of the German Arch-Patriots of 1806-1807*, quoted in Lenin, *Collected Works*, Volume 27 (Moscow, 1972), p494.

4   Niall Ferguson, *The Pity of War* (London, 1998), p462.

5   Mary-Alice Waters (ed), *Rosa Luxemburg Speaks* (New York, 1970), pp235-236.

6   Gary Sheffield, former lecturer, Sandhurst Military Academy, quoted in Neil Davidson's "The Logic of Conflict", *Scottish Left Review*, December 2013.

7   Christopher Clark, *The Sleepwalkers: How Europe Went to War* (London, 2013), p561.

8   Christopher Clark, as above, p562.

9   Quoted from Richard Holmes, *The Western Front* (London, 1999), p13.

10   Adrian Gregory, *The Last Great War* (Cambridge, 2008), p3.

11   Richard Holmes, *The Western Front*, p111.

12   Richard Toye, *Lloyd George and Churchill: Rivals for Greatness* (London, 2007),
     p127.

13   Lenin quoted in Chris Harman, "Marxism and the Missiles", *Socialist Review* (October 1980).

14   Lenin, "Imperialism: The Highest Stage of Capitalism", *Collected Works*, Volume 22 (Moscow 1964), p191.

15   Chris Harman, "Marxism and the Missiles". It is worth noting that, just as Marx drew on the great classical economists David Ricardo and Adam Smith in his analysis of 19th century capitalism, so Lenin and Bukharin used the work of the radical, liberal economist J A Hobson and the Austrian socialist economist Rudolf Hilferding in analysing monopoly capitalism.

16   Chris Harman, "Marxism and the Missiles".

17   Thomas Packenham, *The Scramble for Africa* (London, 1992), p600.

18   See Leo Zeilig, *Patrice Lumumba: Africa's Lost Leader* (London, 2008).

19   Duncan Hallas, *The Meaning of Marxism* (London, 1971), p17.

20   Duncan Hallas, as above, p18.

21   Duncan Hallas, as above, p18.

22   Duncan Hallas, as above, p19.

23   Figures from Gerhard Bry assisted by Charlotte Boschan, *Wages in Germany, 1871-1945* (Princeton, 1960), pp278-279.

Available at http://www.nber. org/chapters/c2510.

24 A Brewer cited in Alex Callinicos, *Imperialism and Global Political Economy* (London, 2009), p26.

25 Chris Harman, *A People's History of the World* (London, 1999), p403.

26 Leon Trotsky, *The War Correspondence; The Balkan Wars 1912-13* (New York, 1981), p15.

27 Leon Trotsky, as above, p15.

28 Paul Foot, *The Vote: How it Was Won and How it Was Undermined* (London, 2012), p213.

29 George Dangerfield, *The Strange Death of Liberal England* (London, 1997), p191.

30 Paul Foot, *The Vote*, p213.

31 Paul Foot, as above, p214.

32 Barbara Drake, *Women in Trade Unions* (London, 1984), p46.

33 Nan Milton (ed), *John Maclean: In the Rapids of Revolution* (London, 1978), p62.

34 John Maclean, *Justice*, 24 February 1912.

35 Christopher Clark, *The Sleepwalkers*, pp488-490.

36 Pierre Broué, *The German Revolution 1917-23* (London, 2006), p9.

37 Tony Cliff, *Rosa Luxemburg* (London, 1980), p14.

38 Pierre Broué, *The German Revolution 1917-23*, p44.

39 Paul Mason, *Live Working or Die Fighting* (London, 2007),

40 Tony Cliff, *Lenin, Volume 2: All Power to the Soviets* (London, 1976), p2.

41 Pierre Broué, *The German Revolution 1917-23*, p44.

42 Leon Trotsky, *My Life* (London, 1975), p243.

43 Stephen Cohen, *Bukharin and the Bolshevik Revolution* (London, 1974), p22.

44 Lenin, "The War and Russian Social Democracy" in *Collected Works*, Volume 21, p23.

45 Lenin, *Collected Works*, Volume 21, p315.

46 Tony Cliff and Donny Gluckstein, *The Labour Party: A Marxist History* (London, 1988), p55.

47 Walter Kendall, *The Revolutionary Movement in Britain* (London, 1969), p88.

48 John Maclean, *Justice*, 17 September 1914.

49 Lenin, *The War and the Second International* (New York, 1932), p9.

50 Duncan Hallas, *The Comintern* (London, 1985), p15.

51 Duncan Hallas, as above, p17.

52 Ken Weller, *Don't be a Soldier! The Radical Anti-war Movement in North London, 1914-1918* (London, 1985), p22.

53 Ralph Miliband, *Parliamentary Socialism* (London, 1972), p44.

54 *Forward*, August 1914, quoted in Walter Kendall, pp110-111.

55 Harry McShane and Joan Smith, *No Mean Fighter* (London, 1978), p63.

56 Lenin, *Collected Works*, Volume 21, p17.

57 Sybil Morrison, a former suffragette, quoted in Lyn Smith, *Voices Against War* (London, 2009), p26.

58 Statistics from Megan Trudell, "Prelude to Revolution", *International Socialism* 76, 1997, p73.

59 William Gallacher, *Revolt on the Clyde* (London, 1978), p18.

60 Leon Trotsky, *My Life*, p240.

61 Chris Harman, *A People's History of the World*, p405.

62 Chris Harman, as above, p406.

63 Harry McShane and Joan Smith, *No Mean Fighter*, p65.

64 David Blackbourn, *The Fontana History of Germany, 1780-1918* (London, 1977), pp461-462.

65 Alexander Shlyapnikov, *On the Eve of 1917* (London, 1982), pp18-19.

66 Ian Birchall, "The Vice Like Hold of Nationalism?", *International Socialism* 78 (Spring 1998), p136.

67 Paul Foot, *The Vote*, p230.

68 Adam Hochschild, *To End All Wars* (London, 2011), p153.

69 Ian Birchall, "The Vice Like Hold of Nationalism?", p135.

70 *Compulsory Military Service: Should the Working Class Support it?* (Socialist Labour Press, 1918), p15.

71 Ian Birchall, "The Vice Like Hold of Nationalism?", p137.

72 Quoted in Ian Birchall, as above.

73 John MacLean, *In the Rapids of Revolution: Essays, Articles and Letters, 1902-23* (Edited by Nan Milton, London, 1978), p88.

74 Ralph Fox, *Smoky Crusade* (London, 1937) cited in Ken Weller, *Don't be a Soldier!*, p38.

75 Harry McShane and Joan Smith, *No Mean Fighter*, p64.

76 William Gallacher, *Revolt on the Clyde*, p37.

77 Chris Harman, *A People's History of the World*, p405.

78 Figures from Megan Trudell, "Prelude to Revolution", p70.

79 Ivan Bloch quoted in Niall Ferguson, *The Pity of War*, pp9-10.

80 Mike Haynes, *Russia: Class and Power 1917-2000* (London, 2002), p9.

81 In December 1916 Asquith resigned and Lloyd George became Prime Minister.

82 David Lloyd George, *War Memoirs of David Lloyd George* (Oldham, 1938), p147.

83 David Lloyd George, as above, p147.

84 Niall Ferguson, *The Pity of War*, p318.

85 Chris Harman, *A People's History of the World*, p409.

86 James Hinton, *The First Shop Stewards' Movement* (London, 1973), pp21-23.

87 Paul Foot, *The Vote*, p235.

88 Lindsey German, *How a Century of War Changed the Lives of Women* (London, 2013), pp26-27.

89 Paul Mason, *Live Working or Die Fighting*, p163.

90 Tony Cliff and Donny

Gluckstein, *Marxism and Trade Union Struggle* (London, 1986), p63.

91 Quoted in Paul Mason, *Live Working or Die Fighting*, pp159, 160.

92 Paul Mason, as above, p163.

93 Paul Mason, as above, p163.

94 Leon Trotsky, *My Life*, p255.

95 Statistics on this page are from H P Willmott, *World War I* (London, 2003), p307.

96 Chris Harman, *A People's History of the World*, p411.

97 Richard Holmes, *The Western Front*, p111.

98 Ian Birchall, "The Vice-like Hold of Nationalism?", p139.

99 Adam Hochschild's narrative from Joe Sacco's *The Great War* (London, 2014).

100 Quoted in Paul O'Flinn, "A Day in the War", *International Socialism* 1:89 (June 1976), p30.

101 Richard Holmes, *The Western Front*, p131.

102 Richard Holmes, as above, p134.

103 Richard Holmes, as above, p139.

104 Richard Holmes, as above, p103.

105 Richard Holmes, as above, p146.

106 Richard Holmes, as above, pp146-147.

107 Cited in Megan Trudell, "Prelude to Revolution", p89.

108 Cited in Megan Trudell, as above, p89.

109 A full account based on interviews with participants is in William Allison and John Fairley, *The Monocled Mutineer* (London, 1979), pp81-111.

110 Nick Howard, "The Shirker's Revolt: Mass Desertion, Defeat and Revolution in the German Army, 1917-20", Conference paper presented to Manchester Metropolitan University, April 1995.

111 Nick Howard, as above.

112 Donny Gluckstein, *The Western Soviets: Workers' Councils versus Parliament 1915-20* (London, 1985), p167.

113 Hew Strachan, *The First World War* (London, 2006), pp112-113.

114 Robert Holland, "The British Empire and the Great War", *The Oxford History of the British Empire*, Volume 4 (Oxford, 1999), p125.

115 Robert Holland, as above, p122.

116 Hew Strachan, *The First World War*, p279.

117 Hew Strachan, as above, p279

118 Hew Strachan, as above, p74.

119 Hew Strachan, as above, p74.

120 See Chris Fuller, "Fighting the War on the Home Front", *Socialist Review* (February 2014), p23.

121 See Steven Johns, http://libcom.org/history/british-west-indies-regiment-mutiny-1918

122 Information and statistics on the Labour Corps from Geoff Bridger, *The Great War Handbook* (Barnsley, 2013), pp163-164.

123 For a full account see Hew Strachan, *The First World*

War, pp107-111. There are two positions that it is important to explicitly reject; the Turkish nationalist one of genocide denial and the more recent phenomenon of using these events to bolster an Islamophobic narrative.

124 Statistics in this paragraph from Megan Trudell, "Prelude to Revolution" p70.

125 Leon Trotsky, *My Life*, p241.

126 James Hinton, *The First Shop Stewards' Movement*, p23.

127 Harry McShane and Joan Smith, *No Mean Fighter*, p62.

128 Ray Challinor, *The Origins of British Bolshevism* (London, 1977), p131.

129 "Fellow Workers"—the Clyde Workers' Committee's first leaflet, summer 1915, https://www.marxists.org/archive/gallacher/1915/clyde-committee.htm

130 William Gallacher, *Revolt on the Clyde*, p51.

131 Ann and Vincent Flynn, *We Shall be All: Recent Chapters on the History of Working Class Struggle in Scotland*, Edited by Laurie Flynn (London, 1978), p24.

132 Tom Bell, *Pioneering Days* (London, 1941), p110.

133 Ray Challinor, *The Origins of British Bolshevism*, p33.

134 B J Ripley and J McHugh, *John Maclean* (Manchester, 1989), p86.

135 Harry McShane and Joan Smith, *No Mean Fighter*, p77.

136 Ray Challinor, *The Origins of British Bolshevism*, p136.

137 Tony Cliff and Donny Gluckstein, *The Labour Party: A Marxist History* (London, 1988), p63.

138 James Connolly writing in *The Irish Worker*, 8 August 1914, quoted in Kieran Allen, *The Politics of James Connolly* (London, 1990), p127.

139 Peter Berresford Ellis, *James Connolly: Selected Writings* (London, 1975), p36.

140 Lenin, *The Right of Nations to Self Determination* (Moscow, 1971), p148.

141 Duncan Hallas, *The Comintern*, p19.

142 Megan Trudell, "Prelude to Revolution", p99.

143 Duncan Hallas, *The Comintern*, p20.

144 Megan Trudell, "Prelude to Revolution", p99.

145 Duncan Hallas, *The Comintern*, p20.

146 Leon Trotsky, *War and the International* (London, 1971), p155.

147 Paul Mason, *Live Working or Die Fighting*, pp163-164.

148 The Revolution began on 23 February according to the Julian calendar, which was 13 days behind the Western Gregorian calendar. Dates in reference to the Russian Revolution are based on the Julian calendar.

149 Mike Haynes, *Russia: Class and Power 1917-2000* (London, 2002), p15.

150 Leon Trotsky, *History of the*

Empire and Revolution

150 Leon Trotsky, *History of the Russian Revolution*, Volume 1 (London, 1967), p109.

151 Cited in Chris Harman, *A People's History of the World*, p413.

152 Leon Trotsky, *History of the Russian Revolution*, Volume 1, p111.

153 Mike Haynes, *Russia*, pp16-17.

154 Megan Trudell, "Prelude to Revolution", p88.

155 Ray Challinor, *The Origins of British Bolshevism*, p187.

156 Nan Milton, *John Maclean* (London, 1973), p9.

157 J Winter and B Baggett, *1914-18: The Great War and the Shaping of the 20th Century* (London, 1996), p278.

158 Figures from Megan Trudell, "Prelude to Revolution", p91.

159 Mike Haynes, *Russia*, p25.

160 Tony Cliff, *Lenin, Volume 2: All Power to the Soviets* (London, 1985), p202.

161 Donny Gluckstein, *The Western Soviets*, pp98-99.

162 Duncan Hallas, *The Comintern*, p21.

163 Chris Harman, *The Lost Revolution: Germany 1918 to 1923* (London, 1982), p30.

164 Donny Gluckstein, *The Western Soviets*, p170.

165 Donny Gluckstein, as above, p170.

166 Mike Haynes, *Russia*, p30.

167 Mike Haynes, as above, p33.

168 Tony Cliff, *Lenin, Volume 2: All Power to the Soviets* (London, 1985), p379.

169 Lenin, quoted in H P Willmott, *World War I*, p230.

170 Hew Strachan, *The First World War*, p257.

171 Lenin quoted in Megan Trudell, "Prelude to Revolution", p92.

172 Chris Harman, *The Lost Revolution*, p31.

173 Paul Broué, *The German Revolution 1917-23*, pp102-103.

174 Chris Harman, *The Lost Revolution*, p31.

175 Chris Harman, as above, p32.

176 Paul Broué, *The German Revolution 1917-23*, p108.

177 Chris Harman, *The Lost Revolution*, p33.

178 Leo Jogiches quoted in Chris Harman, *The Lost Revolution*, p34.

179 Quoted in Donny Gluckstein, *The Western Soviets*, p107.

180 Chris Harman, *The Lost Revolution*, p38.

181 Chris Fuller, "Fighting the War on the Home Front", *Socialist Review* (February 2014), p24.

182 *Solidarity*, paper of the National Shop Stewards and Workers' Committee Movement, February 1918

183 John Foster, "Strike Action and Working Class Politics on Clydeside 1914-19", paper presented at conference on "Working Class Movements and their Revolutionary Potential at the end of WW1", Graz, June 1989.

184 John Foster, as above.

185 John Foster, as above.

186 John Maclean, *In the Rapids of Revolution*, p101.

187 B J Ripley and J McHugh, *John Maclean*, p108.

188 Lenin, *Collected Works*, Volume 27 (Moscow, 1977), p98.

189 Tony Cliff, *Lenin, Volume 3: Revolution Besieged* (London, 1978), p51.

190 Tony Cliff, as above, p50.

191 Figures from Tony Cliff, *Lenin, Volume 3*, p50.

192 Quoted in Chris Harman, *A People's History of the World*, p425.

193 James Hinton, *The First Shop Stewards' Movement*, p17.

194 Chris Harman, *The Lost Revolution*, p39.

195 Hew Strachan, *The First World War*, p257.

196 Nick Howard, "The Shirker's Revolt". Full details of the German mutinies are included in Chapter 7.

197 Chris Harman, *The Lost Revolution*, pp39-40.

198 Nick Howard, "The Shirker's Revolt".

199 Chris Harman, *The Lost Revolution*, p41.

200 Duncan Hallas, *The Meaning of Marxism*, p35.

201 Chris Harman, *The Lost Revolution*, pp48-50

202 John Rose, "Lenin, Luxemburg and the War", *Socialist Review* (April 2014).

203 Peter Nettl, *Rosa Luxemburg* (London, 1960), p725.

204 Paul Frölich, *Rosa Luxemburg* (London, 1994), p285.

205 Mary-Alice Waters (ed), *Rosa Luxemburg Speaks*, pp400-426.

206 Quoted in Chris Harman, *The Lost Revolution*, p68.

207 Lenin, *Left-Wing Communism: An Infantile Disorder* (Moscow, 1970), p36.

208 Paul Frölich, *Rosa Luxemburg*, pp288-289.

209 Chris Harman, *The Lost Revolution*, p75.

210 For details see Paul Frölich, *Rosa Luxemburg*, p292.

211 Chris Harman, *The Lost Revolution*, p74.

212 Chris Harman, "The German Revolution", *Socialist Worker Review* 90 (September 1986).

213 Chris Harman, as above.

214 Chris Harman, *The Lost Revolution*, pp78-80.

215 Paul Levi writing in *Rote Fahne*, 5 September 1920, quoted in Chris Harman, *The Lost Revolution*, p80.

216 Paul Frölich, *Rosa Luxemburg*, p293.

217 *Rote Fahne*, 14 January 1919, cited in Paul Frölich, as above, p299.

218 Leon Trotsky quoted in Chris Harman, "The German Revolution".

219 Nick Howard, "The Social and Political Consequences of the Allied Food Blockade of Germany: 1918-19", University of Sheffield.

220 Quoted in E H Carr, *The Bolshevik Revolution*, Volume 3 (London, 1983), pp135-6.

221 Chris Harman, *A People's History of the World*, p435.

222 E H Carr, *The Bolshevik*

Revolution, p135.

223 Steven Johns, http:libcom.org/ history/british-west-indies-regiments-mutiny-1918.

224 John Newsinger, *The Blood Never Dried: A People's History of the British Empire* (London, 2006), p101.

225 Ray Challinor, *The Origins of British Bolshevism*, p196.

226 Basil Thomson, *The Scene Changes* (London, 1939), p410.

227 *The Times*, 30 January 1919.

228 John Mclean, *In the Rapids of Revolution*, p150.

229 Lord Shinwell, *I've Lived Through It All* (London, 1973), p57.

230 Andrew Rothstein, *The Soldiers' Strikes 1919* (London, 1980), p94.

231 Quoted in Paul O'Flinn, "A Day in the War", *International Socialism* 1:89 (June 1976), p30.

232 Ann and Vincent Flynn, *We Shall be All*, p39.

233 D S Morton, *The Forty Hours Strike* (SLP, 1919), p6.

234 *Glasgow Herald*, January 1919.

235 William Gallacher, *Revolt on the Clyde*, p234.

236 Ann and Vincent Flynn, *We Shall be All*, p44.

237 Aneurin Bevan, *In Place of Fear* (London, 1952), p40.

238 Ray Challinor, *The Origins of British Bolshevism*, p204.

239 James Hinton, *The First Shop Stewards' Movement*, pp13-17.

240 James Hinton, as above, p17.

241 Quoted in Mike Haynes, *Russia*, p46.

242 Paolo Spriano, *The Occupation of the Factories* (London, 1975), p145.

243 Quoted in Chris Harman, *The Lost Revolution*, p306.

244 H P Willmott, *World War I*, p294.

245 Hew Strachan, *The First World War*, p320.

246 John Newsinger, *The Blood Never Dried*, p100.

247 Robert Holland, "The British Empire and the Great War", pp133-134.

248 Robert Holland, as above, pp133-135.

249 Ian MacDougall (ed), *Militant Miners* (Edinburgh, 1981), p12.

250 John Maclean, *The War After the War* (London, 1973), pp25-27.

251 Chris Harman, "Analysing imperialism", *International Socialism* 99 (Summer 2003), pp23-25.

Kieran Allen, *The Politics of James Connolly*, Pluto Press, London, 1990.

Peter Berresford Ellis, *James Connolly: Selected Writings*, Penguin, London, 1975.

Ian Birchall, "The Vice Like Hold of Nationalism?", *International Socialism* 78, spring 1998.

Pierre Broué, *The German Revolution 1917-23*, Merlin Press, London, 2006.

Nicolai Bukharin, *Imperialism and World Economy*, Bookmarks, London, 2003.

Alex Callinicos, *Imperialism and Global Political Economy*, Polity Press, London, 2009.

E H Carr, *The Bolshevik Revolution*, Volume 3, Harmondsworth, London, 1966.

Ray Challinor, *The Origins of British Bolshevism*, Croom Helm, London, 1977.

Christopher Clark, *The Sleepwalkers: How Europe Went to War*, Penguin Books, London, 2013.

Tony Cliff, *Rosa Luxemburg*, Bookmarks, London, 1980.

Tony Cliff, *Lenin, Volume 2: All Power to the Soviets*, Bookmarks, London, 1976.

Tony Cliff, *Lenin, Volume 3: Revolution Besieged*, Pluto Press, London, 1978.

Tony Cliff and Donny Gluckstein, *The Labour Party: A Marxist History*, Bookmarks, London, 1988.

Tony Cliff and Donny Gluckstein, *Marxism and Trade Union Struggle*, Bookmarks, London, 1986.

George Dangerfield, *The Strange Death of Liberal England*, Serif, London, 1997.

Neil Davidson, "The Logic of Conflict", *Scottish Left Review*, December 2013.

Paul Foot, *The Vote: How it Was Won and How it Was Undermined*, Bookmarks, London, 2012.

Paul Frölich, *Rosa Luxemburg*, Bookmarks, London, 1994.

William Gallacher, *Revolt on the Clyde*, Lawrence & Wishart, London, 1978.

Lindsey German, *How a Century of War Changed the Lives of Women*, Pluto Press, London, 2013.

Donny Gluckstein, *The Western Soviets*, Bookmarks, London, 1985.

Duncan Hallas, *The Meaning of Marxism*, Pluto Press, London, 1971.

Duncan Hallas, *The Comintern*, Bookmarks, London, 1985.

Chris Harman, *A People's History of the World*, Verso, London, 2008.

Chris Harman, "Marxism and the Missiles" (1980). http://www.marxists.org/archive/harman/1980/10/missiles.html.

Chris Harman, *The Lost Revolution: Germany 1918 to 1923*, Bookmarks, London, 1997.

Chris Harman, "Analysing imperialism", *International Socialism* 99, summer 2003.

Chris Harman, "The German Revolution", *Socialist Worker Review* 90, September 1986.

Mike Haynes, *Russia: Class and Power 1917-2000*, Bookmarks, London, 2002.

James Hinton, *The First Shop Stewards' Movement*, George Allen & Unwin, London, 1973.

Adam Hochschild, *To End All Wars*, Houghton Mifflin Harcourt, London, 2011.

Robert Holland, "The British Empire and the Great War", *The Oxford History of the British Empire*, Vol 4, OUP, Oxford, 1999.

Richard Holmes, *The Western Front*, BBC Worldwide, London, 1999.

V I Lenin, *Left-Wing Communism: An Infantile Disorder*, Progress Publishers, Moscow, 1970

V I Lenin, *The War and the Second International*, International Publishers, New York, 1932.

V I Lenin, *The Right of Nations to Self Determination*, Progress Publishers, Moscow, 1971.

Mary-Alice Waters (ed), *Rosa Luxemburg Speaks*, Pathfinder Press, New York, 1970.

John Maclean, *The War After the War*, Socialist Reproduction, London, 1973.

Paul Mason, *Live Working or Die Fighting*, Harvill Secker, London, 2007.

Harry McShane and Joan Smith, *No Mean Fighter*, Pluto Press, London, 1978.

Nan Milton (ed), *John Maclean: In the Rapids of Revolution*, Alison & Busby, London, 1978.

John Newsinger, *The Blood Never Dried: A People's History of the British Empire*, Bookmarks, London 2006.

B J Ripley & J McHugh, *John Maclean*, Manchester University Press, 1989.

Andrew Rothstein, *The Soldiers' Strikes 1919*, Palgrave MacMillan, London, 1980.

Joe Sacco, *The Great War*, Jonathan Cape, London, 2013.

Dave Sherry, *John Maclean: Red Clydesider*, Bookmarks, London, 2014.

Paolo Spriano, *The Occupation of the Factories*, Pluto Press, London, 1975.

Hew Strachan, *The First World War*, Pocket Books, London, 2006.

Leon Trotsky, *My Life*, Pathfinder Press, New York, 1971.

Leon Trotsky, *The War Correspondence of Leon Trotsky; The Balkan Wars 1912-13*, Pathfinder, New York, 1981.

Leon Trotsky, *War and the International*, Wesley Press, London, 1971.

Leon Trotsky, *History of the Russian Revolution*, Volume 1, Sphere, London, 1967.

Leon Trotsky, *Problems of Everyday Life*, Pathfinder Press, New York, 1973.

Megan Trudell, "Prelude to Revolution: Class Consciousness and the First World War", *International Socialism* 76, autumn 1997.

Ken Weller, *Don't be a Soldier!* Journeyman Press/London History Workshop, 1986. https://libcom.org/history/dont-be-soldier-radical-anti-war-movement-north-london-1914-1918-ken-weller

INDEX

Empire and Revolution